JAMES HOGG

James Hogg was b̶ ̶ ̶ ̶ ̶ ̶ ̶ ̶ ̶ ̶ ̶ ̶ ̶ ̶ ̶ ̶ ̶ ̶art of
Ettrick Forest and r̶ ̶ ̶ ̶ ̶ ̶ ̶ ̶ ̶ ̶ ̶ ̶ ̶ ̶ ̶ ̶ ̶ ̶ge of
seven he spent most ̶ ̶ ̶ ̶ ̶ ̶ ̶ ̶ ̶ ̶ ̶ ̶ ̶ ̶ ̶the
surrounding hills and ̶ ̶ ̶ ̶ ̶ ̶ ̶ ̶ ̶ ̶ ̶ ̶ ̶, compos-
ing verses after the st̶ ̶ ̶ ̶ ̶ ̶ ̶ ̶ ̶ ̶ads learned from
his mother. 'Jamie the̶ ̶ ̶ ̶ ̶ ̶ ̶ ̶e was soon known, wrote
songs for the lasses to s̶ ̶ ̶ ̶d sent some that he had learnt to
the Sheriff of Selkirkshire, Mr. Walter Scott, then compiling his
"Border Minstrelsy". In 1803, 'The Ettrick Shepherd' published his first collection of poems and songs, "The Mountain
Bard" and, for several years, tried to combine farming and
writing, but with little success. In 1810, disillusioned, James
Hogg arrived in Edinburgh and determined to make his reput-
ation as a literary man. Finding little enthusiasm for his talents
and as few offers of employment, he launched a weekly paper,
"The Spy", and gained some notoriety from the risque tales
which he wrote for it. His fortunes fluctuated from then on and,
despite many setbacks which he largely attributed to the literary
establishment's hostility towards an outsider lacking in title or
degree, Hogg produced a considerable body of work and won an
assured place in society. After abandoning verse in disgust, he
concentrated his energies on a series of novels and his talents
found their fullest expression in the powerful and shocking
"Confessions of a Justified Sinner" — so heretical was this
work considered that it was some time before its author dared
identify himself. James Hogg spent his later years back in the
Borders, in the little cottage at Altrive, given to him by the Duke
of Buccleuch. And it was there that he died on November 22nd
1835. He is commemorated by a fine monument which over-
looks St. Mary's Loch and Tibbie Shiel's famous Inn where the
shepherd and his literary contemporaries spent many a con-
vivial evening.

James Hogg
HIGHLAND
TOURS

The Ettrick Shepherd's Travels
in the Scottish Highlands and
Western Isles in 1802, 1803 and 1804
with an Introduction by
SIR WALTER SCOTT

Edited by William F. Laughlan

Byways

First published 1981 by Byway Books
9 Maxton Court, Hawick, Roxburghshire TD9 7QN

© **Byway Books**

ISBN 0 907448 00 3

Phototypeset in Compugraphic English 18
and Printed in Scotland by Kelso Graphics,
The Knowes, Kelso, Roxburghshire.

PUBLISHER'S NOTE

While James Hogg was certainly an observant and well-
informed traveller, and in many respects a meticulous reporter,
he suffered from a tendency common among his contemporaries
— and still to be found — towards a cavalier disrespect for
spelling and facts. We have retained his versions of both
throughout this edition and appeal to observant readers not to
draw our attention to such discrepancies as the height of Ben
Nevis or the spelling of Ettrick. We owe it to our printers to
make this statement and trust that the curiosities which occur
will appeal to your good-humour, discernment and imagination.

CONTENTS

Maps

Illustrations

All illustrations courtesy of Borders Regional Council Library Service.

EDITOR'S NOTE

This is not a scholarly work. My intention in editing James Hogg's letters, which originally appeared in serialised form in literary journals of the 19th century, was to make them available to a wider readership; to permit the modern traveller to turn back the clock and see those same mountains and glens, towns and lochs, through the eyes of the young Ettrick Shepherd. A contemporary of Sir Walter Scott, though from a very different background, Hogg saw Scotland quite differently from his patron — and his views may not accord with some of those prevalent today. But that, to me, is part of their strength: James Hogg was not writing with hindsight, or to glamourise. Never one to hide his own genius, he expresses his true feelings — on people, politics, religion and art — without regard for the beliefs of his reader. We may not agree with him, but we can relish his honesty.

This then, is a work to be enjoyed. But it is also meant to be used — for the letters describe the routes which James Hogg actually followed, in sunshine and rain, and which can still be taken. They are routes which traverse some of the most dramatic and beautiful landscapes in Europe and took the young writer from his Border home, through scenes hallowed in legend, to the Western Isles.

Indeed, he intended to settle on Harris and, before leaving on the 1804 journey wrote and published his "Farewell to Ettrick". But plans fell through and Hogg was forced to swallow his own pride. He dubbed that last expedition "the terrible journey" but still managed to retain his sense of humour and laugh at his own folly.

And that balance between good-natured egotism and tongue-in-cheek self criticism helped sustain James Hogg. He was always ready to play his part as an uncouth, unmannered shepherd, allowing his "betters" to think themselves betters. But behind that facade, Hogg knew his capabilities and was never afraid to speak his mind.

I hope that this book, then, will remind people of a Scottish writer who has been somewhat forgotten and of a Scotland that has, in many respects, changed little. Perhaps a discovery of the two together will prove a rewarding experience.

I must thank, for their help, the Borders Region Library Service, the staff of Hawick Library and, in particular, Hugh Mackay and Liz Robinson. For their patience, I am ever grateful to my wife, Ann, and my daughters, Emily and Frances.

7

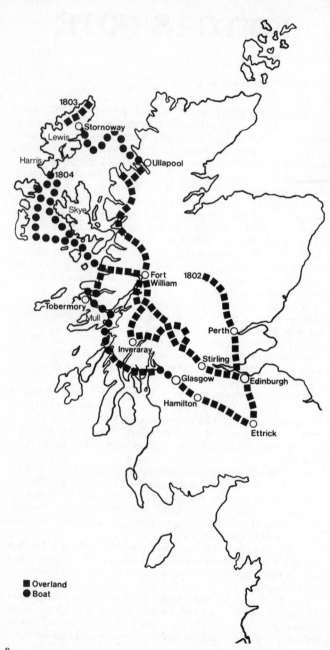

1803

Stornoway

Lewis

Harris

1804

Skye

Ullapool

Fort William

Tobermory

Mull

Inveraray

1802

Perth

Stirling

Glasgow

Edinburgh

Hamilton

Ettrick

■ Overland
● Boat

8

INTRODUCTION

To the Editor of the Scots Magazine.

*Edinburgh,
26th Sept. 1802.*

Sir,
The inclosed letter is the first of a series received by me from a young man born in Ettrick Forest, and literally bred there in the humble situation of a shepherd. Various causes have concurred, in Scotland, to excite and encourage acuteness of observation, and strength of character, even among those who have reaped few or no advantages from fortune and from education. From the remarks of such men, especially upon subjects which they have been accustomed to consider with accuracy, more information may be derived than perhaps the pride of lettered rank will readily allow.

We often hear the trite remark, that a stranger usually sees more of a town which he visits upon his travels, than those who have all their life been its inhabitants. Something like this may occur in the fields of knowledge. Those whose education has commenced with the first opening of their ideas, who have never known what it was to be at large from the trammels of an instructor, who have been as it were, "rocked and cradled, and dandled" into men of literature, may be considered as the denizens of the realms of taste and science. But the uneducated and hardy intruder, whose natural strength of mind impels him to study, and to whose researches novelty gives all its charms, may, while bewildering himself in unknown streets, and occasionally mistaking gewgaws and trinkets for real treasures, view nevertheless recesses untrod before, and discover beauties neglected by those who have been bred up among them.

I felt myself deeply impressed with the truth of those observations, on perusing part of the journal which my correspondent had kept during a distant highland tour, and at my request, he undertook to digest his travelling observations into a series of letters. Should you think them worthy of a place in your Publication I should hope many of your readers may be amused, and even instructed, in following the views and ideas of such a character as I have described, especially when I assure you, that it is not assumed to give a factitious interest to the letters, which are really and unaffectedly the production of a shepherd of Ettrick Forest.

I remain, Sir, Your humble servant,

Walterscott

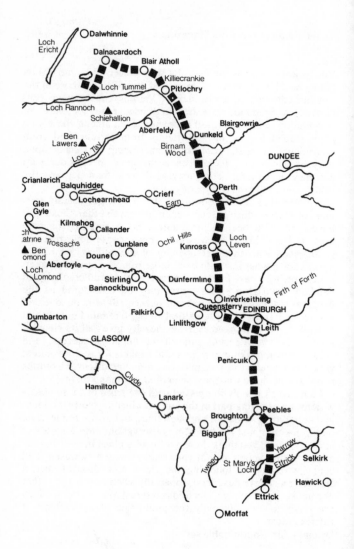

1802

Dear Sir — As you desired me, I am now to give you an account of my journey thro' the North Highlands and I am afraid you will be much disappointed in the perusal. Were it not, indeed, that I know you admire nature most when most simply dressed, I should not at all have attempted it; but encouraged by this, I will endeavour to lead your eyes to every scene over which mine wander with amazement — whether of majestical deformity, or natural elegance; and though I am conscious how greatly deficient my intelligence shall be; it being merely an outside view of things which I am enabled to present, I have the satisfaction, however, of being assured that I am communicating them to a mind capable of giving every hint its full expansion.

But as you will expect me to describe, as I go along, I must tell you what sort of a place Etterick is. If you already know, you may divert yourself by comparing this with the impression engraven on your own remembrance; and if you do not, it is time you did. At any rate, it will form a striking contrast with other countries which we must immediately survey.

The name Etterick is of great antiquity. The Gaelic term, from which I am told it is derived, hath some reference to darkness; and it is believed to have been descriptive of sylvan scenery, rather of a dismal nature — probably in the near neighbourhood of the parish church, as it is there only that sundry places are thus particularized as Old Etterick-hill, Etterick-house, Etterick-hall, Etterick-pen, although the whole country is termed Etterick Forest.

The hills are generally of a beautiful deep green, thick covered with sheep, though no-wise rugged or tremendous. The highest is Phauppenn, which rises 2370 feet above the level of the sea. The view from the top of this mountain is very extensive to the south and east, but northwards is immediately intercepted by the interposition of Hertfell and the White Coom, betwixt which the palm has been disputed as the highest in Scotland south of the Forth — though it certainly belongs to the latter. Its elevation above the sea being 2840 feet.

The view from this mountain is truly astonishing and is, I believe, unequalled in Britain. To the north-east and southwest, it is lost in the German and Irish seas; all round, to the south and east at prodigious distances, rise the fells of Cockermouth, Skiddaw, Cheviot and Lammermoor; and in the interstices between these it is lost in space.

The afternoon, when the sun is well about, is the time for a view southward, when all the countries that lye betwixt these mountains with their varied scenery, are seen at one glance. But the rugged grandeur of the scene almost immediately below your feet soon attracts the eye and draws all the attention.

There, you see Loch Skene with its surrounding rocks which have been, time out of mind, the impregnable refuge of the fox, the eagle and all the other beasts and birds of prey known in these countries.

There, you see the famous cataract called the Grey-mare's-tail (overhung by the Bubbly craig on the one side and Turn-berry on the other) which falls, with only one small inter-mission, near 300 feet.

The contemplation of these objects naturally fills the mind with dismal and melancholy ideas; but you only have to lift your eyes to behold the cheering and enlivening prospect of a large extent of country, flourishing in peace and plenty, and all the corners of the world pouring in their commerce on each side of you.

Here I will leave you to your own reflections during the night and, if you awake in time the next morning and the sky clear, you will see the smoke rising in many a small streamer out of the city of Glasgow and, beyond that, the sovereigns of the north headed by Ben Lomond, like a regiment of blue pyramids, towering their everlasting tops behind one another, vying with emulation, who shall be the first to bid good-morrow to the sun.

But this is taking the near cut to the Highlands with a vengeance; so I must, after begging your pardon for this disgression which I am careless whether you grant or not, return to Etterick which I left abruptly from the top of Phaup-penn.

The river Etterick taketh its rise five miles S.S.E. of the village of Moffat and runs a course of 30 miles. About a mile and an half above Selkirk it is augmented one half by the tribute of its sister Yarrow; and as far below that ancient burgh, the Tweed is increased nearly one half by these united streams.

The two rivers, Etterick and Yarrow, form properly what is called Etterick Forest — which was the Sylva Caledonia of the ancients and is now the Arcadia of Britain, the whole scene, life and manners of the inhabitants being truly pastoral.

In the upper parts of the country small indeed are the remains of the wood with which it once was wholly covered; but in the lower parts there is some, both natural and planted. The district abounds with old towers which, in their time, had been places of strength; and there is not one in ten that hath not some time been inhabited by the Scots, branches of the family of Buccleuch.

The lives of the principal shepherds, for so I denominate the store-farmers, are very easy and to those who can relish such a life, elegant and agreeable. They delight greatly in poetry and music, in which sundry are considerable proficients. Burns's are the favourite songs and the Scottish strathspeys the favourite music. Their more quiet and retired diversions are cards, the dam-board and backgammon.

The manners of the common people are truly singular, from their simplicity. They have generally the musical ear, are passionately fond of songs and, for variety, greatly excel their superiors. The good-man's library oft-times consists of a family Bible, Boston's *Four-fold State of Man,* and a large sheaf or two of ballads. In no place are there so many old songs, tales and anecdotes preserved by tradition; whilst the new ones are early introduced, being sought for with such avidity — each one being fond of something new to divert the social circle.

Many of Burns's songs and McNeil's were sung and admired long before we knew who were the authors; and with pride I relate it, many popular songs and tunes are indebted to the Forest for the first discovery of their excellence. Yet we have not a noted composer of music amongst us, our best modern tunes being of Perthshire original.

In no part of the south of Scotland hath the ancient superstitions so long kept their ground. The fairies have but lately and reluctantly quitted its green holms and flowery glens. Gaists and bogles are as plenty as ever — not potato bogles, my dear Sir, but awful, terrible bogles who assume the most fantastical shapes and play the maddest like actions which the most whimsical spirits can invent. I could tell you fifty stories of the causes of these apparitions, of their laying and how vilely they have fooled some of our parsons.

You will think this is no very favourable picture of a country which is beginning to emerge into notice, where indeed there are many very sensible people and where the youth, as you know, have made great proficiency in the arts and sciences, as well as in trade and manufactures. The fact is, the Forest being surrounded by high mountains remained long excluded from any intercourse with the more fertile districts surrounding these; even to this day the cross roads are in a state of nature. The consequence of all this was a later and more sudden emergence from barbarity; and so used have the people, even of this generation, been to hear these stories told as authentic by the very persons whom they were bound by nature to believe and obey, that you may as well think to argue them out of the belief of their own existence as of their authenticity.

But if we go on at this rate we will not reach the Highlands this season.

About ten years ago, I had occasion to make a jaunt through the west of Stirlingshire, Monteith, Breadalbane and Glenorchy, in which district — as you well know — there are striking views of Grampian scenery, as are anywhere to be met with. Here too, I found the economy of sheep farming; not, as I had expected, in its infancy, but managed with as much success and care as the same species of sheep were south of the Tweed. And as no body told me otherwise, I returned fully convinced that the whole Highlands, as far as John O' Groats House, were stocked in the same manner; and hence formed conclusions with regard to the state of our markets very different from the result.

Last year, again, I took another journey through the eastern parts of the Grampian Hills, penetrating as far as the sources of the Dee, where I beheld large tracts of fine pasture countries appropriated to — I know not what, unless to the benefit of such wild beasts of the field and fowls of the heaven, as are pleased to make them resting places.

I gathered, however, as much information as furnished good matter of discourse with my country neighbours for a twelvemonth and some stories that, with a little colouring, made them stare exceedingly. Consulting several tours through Scotland, I found in none of them any observations on the great neglect of sheep-stock, which is our chief staple commodity and the only animal, for the rearing of which a great part of Scotland seems designed by nature.

My own remarks being in time worn threadbare and being unable to recruit them from the observations of others, I resolved upon a more extensive circuit; I will not begin another sheet, for fear of doubling your postage, but subscribe myself, Yours for ever,

James Hogg

Candle-maker-row
Friday 23rd July 1802

Dear Sir — in addition to my last I intended to have inserted some sketches relating to the history of the Forest and the means of its improvement, but feared you would think I had forgot the subject of which I professed to give you an account. According to my resolve, I left Ettrick on the 23rd of July 1802 and took the road by Blackhouse and Peebles for Edinburgh.

On reaching the Tweed and, it being the spawning season, all hands were employed about the flocks. The blooming maids ascended to the ewes milking evening and morning, while the weary shepherd was glad to catch the small interval from employment and take a nap beside his faithful curan, on the green turf of the bught.

In less than half an hour after leaving the Forest's precincts, I entered the burgh of Peebles, by a strong old bridge of five arches over the Tweed. Some are of the opinion that it was built by Alexander III in conjunction with the people of the town; but there is a tradition prevails in Tweeddale, of its having been built by a great lady, and that the builders had their choice of a plack or a peck of meal, as their days wage. A modern need not wonder at this — if you were giving me the value of any thing, you might safely give me my choice of a worse thing; but when he hears that only one-third of the masons accepted of the meal, it somewhat startles him. At such a distance hath time removed their proportional value, that the mind recoils at swallowing the improbability. Pray, dear Sir, you who read a great many old books, try to discover by the price of the meal in what reign the bridge was built.

The town of Peebles is pleasantly situated upon two ridges, on the north bank of the river Tweed, whose pure limpid waters flow near it — sometimes in the most gentle meanders, in other places incessantly foaming in grand yet terrific weills.

The water of Eddleston, over which there are two bridges, intersects and divides the town, whose waters — soiled with the tannage emit a noxious effluvia, especially in warm weather.

Excepting this, Peebles is a most healthy and pleasant situation. The soil is dry; the air, passing through the mountains from all directions, is pure and ventilated; the roads good and the waters salubrious; and though at such a distance inland, its elevation is not above 560 feet above the level of the sea.

It is in a flourishing state, both as to population, manufactures and repair. Its churches are worthy of notice. The high church, which was dedicated to the Virgin Mary, standing at the head of the old town, is a structure of great antiquity; the date of its foundation no man can discover; but it had been thoroughly repaired and endowed in the 11th century, when the ambitious bishops of Rome were forming designs of universal spiritual empire. On a rising ground, at the back of the old town, is situated the Cross Kirk — so denominated, not from its situation but because it was dedicated to the Holy Cross; it is a stupendous fabric, built in the gothic stile, and yet so entire as to be quite defined. It was built by Alexander III in the year 1260. The modern church and steeple surpass, in elegance, those of any other country town that I ever saw.

Peebles is much ornamented and profited by the vicinity of sundry beautiful villas, inhabited by families of distinction. At a small distance from the head of the old town stands the strong and antient castle of Nedpath; strong and antient indeed it is, for its walls are about twelve feet in thickness, and the lime and whinstone so strongly cemented, as to be rendered one solid mass; nor can it be less than 700 years since its erection. Here, at an early period, resided the chief of the powerful clan of the Frazers, the ancestors of the families of Lovat and Salton in the north. Here the gallant and patriotic Sir Simon Frazer defended himself, in the time of Wallace's struggle with the too powerful English monarch. Here he once entertained that hero, with his little band, in a liberal manner, and often assisted and befriended him. To the intrepid bravery and steady performance of this knight was it chiefly owing, that the Scots gained the signal victory of Roslin — where an army only of 10,000 headed by him and Cuming defeated 30,000 English in three desperate actions. From this chief are descended, in the female line, the families of the Marquis of Tweeddale and the Earl of Wigton — as the blending of their arms (exclusive of more substantial proof) can testify. It is probable that the Frazers, in those early ages, had been benefactors to Peebles, for the arms of the family are to be seen on the cross to this day.

On leaving Peebles I ascended Eddleston water, passed the village of Eddleston, hard by which stands the elegant house of Darnhall, surrounded with wood — a seat of Lord Elibank's — and reached the confines of Lothian without seeing or meeting any thing worthy of notice.

On my right rose high mountains all over green, being the western extremity of that range which terminates above Dunbar; these have a beautiful appearance compared with their eastern parts, the bleak and dreary ridges of Lammermuir. On my left the country was more flat and my view more extended, the soil cold but well fertilized with lime.

The country of Tweeddale which I now left is like the Forest, in every sense of the word *pastoral:* it being one large chain of mountains which are, however, everywhere intersected by waters winding through them to join the Tweed; on the sides of these, extensive and well cultivated vallies stretch themselves. The hills on the north of the river are clothed with a beautiful verdure; those on the south have a black and highland appearance.

The principal stock on these mountains is still the Scotish black faced sheep and they are well known for a hardy and healthy race: the more fine wooled breeds are adopted on some farms in the eastern part of the country, inhabited by an active and discerning tenantry. It is probable indeed that these mountains would not raise them to such a size as the more southern grassy districts would, but they would maintain greater numbers, reckoning by the rent. The fleeces would be excellent and the sheep themselves hardy and durable would, in wet seasons, outsell those on soft lands in our stock markets.

The only difficulty and danger lies in the first change; when once the Cheviot breed become the natives of a soil there is no difference, save in the lambing season, for which I reckon the farmer fully compensated by the difference in price — exclusive of the prodigious prices at present given for the fine wool which I hope will open the farmer's eyes to his own real profit.

The farmers of Tweeddale are very wealthy, possess large tracts of land and are the most haughty race of men of that class that are, I believe, in Britain. The Commonalty, both in town and country parts, are sober and industrious, particularized for a strict observance of the Sabbath and a steady attendance on Divine ordinances.

I now reached Kingside edge and, the day being fine, had a fine view of the Firth of Forth, with the numerous towns and villages on its shores; the extensive carse of Lothian waving with a most luxuriant and promising crop, raised in my mind pleasant reflections on the bounties of providence to this favoured isle.

Descending a long declivity, I reached the village of Howgate, the stage and about midway between Peebles and Edinburgh. Here I halted a little and proceeded slowly on until nearly opposite Pennycuik where, on a muir which I think they call Pomathorn, I beheld a numerous croud, male and female, on horseback and on foot, intermixed without order or regularity. I could not conceive what occasion called out such numbers.

Observing strange dresses I expected instantly to see a Merry Andrew, but a stir beginning to rise they drew off in detached numbers. I now anticipated a review of the military and jogged on, looking eagerly forward, until accosted by a loud shout from the crowd to clear the way; drawing my bridle to learn what it meant, I was informed by one nearer me that I was desired to be so good as to take one side of the road, which I did, joining a solitary gentleman on horseback — but observing his eyes rivetted toward that part of the muir where the multitude was thickest, I looked the same way.

The mystery was now cleared up: several horses started for a race and, after running thrice round a certain course on the muir, one of them — a small, handsome galloway — won.

I then ventured to ask the gentleman if he knew whether there were to be any more and was told there was another to start in a few minutes, that if I would wait, he would accompany me to Leith for, owing to the tide going out so late we could easily get there time enough for the race.

I acquiesced and enquired about the origin of the races we were now viewing. He said they were put out by a club of boys, each paying so much annually to a box or common stock, for the support of such members as should be reduced by sickness or misfortune, that this was a holiday with them (the anniversary of their club he supposed), that they would spend the evening in foot races and dancing, that these were the members so fantastically dressed with ribbons which they had got from neighbouring girls whom they, in return, would treat at their ball in the evening; that there had lately been another day of diversion by the whipmen — another and stronger club — at which the farmers grudged, as it took all their servants from work.

The second race was now announced by the drum, when a black horse and a brown started; the latter was always behind until near the goal, when he sprung by and won the race, contrary to my expectation.

They then rode off with a sort of regularity, two men at rank preceded by the drum; the members were all most all on horses, some of which were very lean. I never in all my life saw ribbons more unfitly matched than on some of the riders; they seemed to have only one suit of clothes and, the day being warm, many of them had left their stockings and shoes behind them. I would not have given forty shillings for man, horse, raiment and furniture — one half of which I rate as the value of the ribbons.

As my comrade was far from being communicative, little more passed in our way to Leith, where we arrived just in time enough to see the last heat, which was won by a black mare belonging to the Duke of Hamilton.

Scarcely had I arrived at my lodgings in the Candle-maker-row, and disposed of my horse for the night, when I encountered several acquaintances of my own country, on their way to the theatre. Although I felt myself strongly inclined for some refreshment, having got no dinner, I relinquished it for the sake of their company during the evening — promising myself the highest entertainment from that and the stage, a performance which I had never but once seen before.

We seated ourselves about the middle of the pit and I was more highly diverted by the shrewd remarks of Mr. A. P. who sat next to me, than with any thing I saw or heard that night. The play was *The Heir at Law* which I had never read, consequently can make few remarks on it; but, as an illiterate countryman's opinions of the play and actors are very likely to be quite different from that of every other person I cannot resist the impulse of telling you mine in broad Scotch.

In short, then, Mr. Rock is my favourite actor — so singularly does he mould his features and action to the occasion, that he however missed the desired occasion on me; and I really believe that, in any whimsical character, this old fellow is an adept; besides, he speaks with an audible voice which is an article of greater importance than many of them seem to be aware of, and in a language which I perfectly understood; the dialect of most of them, being so much infected with the Northumberland burr, was much the same to me as the Highland Gaelic. This they possibly do from affection and in order to appear quite grand.

Mr. Weston pleased me exceedingly in the character of Ezekiel Homespun; he acted some parts in the very same way an honest peasant would have done naturally on the same occasions; but on any excess of joy he was by far too fulsome. In particular, when he got the prize in the lottery, had he then put on a mask of the most affected indifference, taking care that his extravagant joy should now and then appear through, it would surely have been more in character than leaping and roaring and singing, disregarding everything else but his great luck. But upon the whole, Mr. Weston acted well: but like yourself I inherit the singular propensity of picking faults with everything that pleaseth me.

There was one Mr. H. Johnston, often saluted with loud claps and bursts of applause: I was very glad to see the people so well pleased for, excepting a becoming assurance, I could detect no excellency in his performance. I joined heartily in applauding his wife; she was so beautiful I could not help it. She supported the character of the English captive in the *Sultan*, which was added as an afterpiece, with great life.

I have often read of the moderation of an Edinburgh audience and that it was the safest place for either a middling play, or player, to make their first appearance; but the contrary was verified here tonight. A Mr. Mordaunt appeared for the first time on the stage — I thought the goodness of his person and the misfortunes of the character which he represented might at least have claimed a patient hearing, but all was in vain — no sooner had he and Mr. Mullender entered than the buzz began, which continued to grow louder and more bitter at every entrance and exit. They never staid to see whether they were going to act well or ill. The men were put entirely out of countenance, blundering their parts and blushing like crimson, nor was it any wonder — unless they were bred innkeepers, — it was impossible they could stand it.

Mr. Mullender entered afterwards in the character of the Sultan, when so loud grew the buzz of disapprobation that he stopped, appealing to the audience how it was possible he could proceed whilst so insulted and offered to desist. This had the desired effect: he was called to proceed from all corners, which he did, and was no more found fault with.

Being obliged to wait on some people in town before I proceed northward, I find that in preferring an amusement to my other concerns I have frustrated my design of reaching Kinross next night. Still, I thought there might be a possibility of abridging my visits and riding there on the afternoon; but on hearing *Hamlet* announced for next evening, I determined to stay another day in Edinburgh and do everything with deliberation, steadfastly remaining, your

Ettrick Shepherd

Candle-maker-row
Saturday 24th July

Dear Sir — Mr. William Laidlaw being newly returned from an excursion of the same nature, he absolutely refused to accompany me; he however informed me that Mr. Andrew Mercer, a man about my own age, who was a painter, a poet and a philosopher and born and bred by the side of my own native stream, intended a jaunt through the Highlands — and even the very road which I then proposed taking: I hasted to his lodgings — He could not go!

I had the mortification now to discover that my credulity had brought me to the alternative of delaying my journey until late in Autumn, or making it alone; the former of which I had nearly resolved on before I called on your worship, whose remonstrances soon determined me to proceed.

There were sundry other gentlemen whom I thought it incumbent on me to see, but though I shortened my visits exceedingly, I saw not half of them. Not being acquainted with the cross lanes, I take a weary time to traverse Edinburgh; before I can find a place that I want, I generally walk thrice as much as I need to do; and if I find it — which is not always the case — my intellectual powers are commonly so much disordered by fatigue and heat that I seldom relish their conversation so much as their drink.

Having spent the fore-part of the day in this manner, I went down on foot to Leith to see the race, which was a good one: Logie o' Buchan beating the other only a very small space. On coming in, however, they both foundered, threw the riders, hurt one of them considerably, and knocked down a poor boy. I saw him carried by me in the greatest agony and, as I believed, on the borders of eternity; I felt extremely for him and wished for his sake that there had been no race that day.

There was another one by four or five horses in the intervals; they were very unequally matched and caused much laughing. They afforded very small entertainment to me, far less than did a blind fiddler whom I encouraged to stay near me and play some of my favourite tunes, by dropping halfpence to him now and then.

I would not exchange a sight of a foot race by half-a-dozen stark shepherds for all the horse races I ever saw; in the different emotions painted in lively colours on the faces of each of the former, the human heart partakes; the feelings are interested; whilst their various manoeuvres constitute a subject of mirth for a length of time. I could make nothing this way of the horse; the only sensations I felt were rather unpleasant. I pitied the poor animals that were strained at such a rate and trembled for the riders, who were cleaving the atmosphere with a velocity I had never before witnessed — saving in the bolt that precedes the peal of thunder; even the Lochskene eagle, in all her pride, methought, could scarcely have kept above their heads.

The crowd was prodigious. I never expected to see so many people together in this world and many of them, I am sure, knew not for what they were come together, there being thousands on the sands betwixt the carriages and the scaffolds that could not see the heads of the riders. I was, however, particularly satisfied, believing it to be the issue of an ugly

dream which I had on a preceding night and which I took for the
outline of a far more terrible and sublime event. I dreamed of
such crowds! nothing but people as far as the eye could reach
and, awakening in trepidation, the impression sat heavy on my
mind: I was going what I counted a long journey and knew not
the consequences — but I was now satisfied that what I took for
a visionary perspective of the day of judgment had only been
one of Leith races!

The only other things that I noticed on my way to and from
Leith were two men with each a handful of printed papers, the
contents of which they were crying nearly as follows, "A true
list of all the ladies, &c. &c." I was shocked at this open
violation of decency — such an advertisement I had never heard
before: but I hope they were not such ladies as I really took them
for.

Immediately below the Circus, at the head of the walk, there
is a small pavement for foot passengers over which the carts
were constantly crossing. There, stood a tall meagre figure,
with a besom nearly as long as himself, sweeping the pavement
at the approach of any well dressed people, then taking off his
hat, he bowed low, presenting it to receive what they were
pleased to give him for his pains.

Farther down, on the same side, stood a mutilated figure of a
sailor, in the same humbling attitude. I eyed them both, but
having no halfpence I resolved to give them something on my
return: it is a very small pittance indeed that my circumscribed
fortune, if a few scores of sheep may be called a fortune, can
afford in charity; but I never pass one that asks it without giving
something if I have it. I cannot suffer a craving look from a dog,
but when a fellow mortal intercedes who is, perhaps, in every
other aspect a better man than myself; Good God! can I, can any
person, refuse what is of such small value to him? I'll tell you
my dear Sir, what you may do for an experiment, for I know your
heart is "tender to the last degree" — the next poor, ragged,
emaciated wretch that begs your charity, try to put yourself in
his place, from which it is out of the power of present affluence
to exempt you in the inconstant affairs of life. Believe this for a
little and you will find how it will melt you.

Accordingly, I came up the same road, the sailor bowed and I
gave him his penny. I walked slowly bye my long man with the
besom — he stood as upright as the shaft of his instrument! — I
kept my penny. He had his eyes fixed upon some ladies and
gentlemen who were coming hand in hand up behind me. He
swept the road and bowed low to them — they gave him
nothing! — you had as good have bowed to me, friend, said I to
myself and walked off, laughing at my own silliness and quest-
ioning much the source of my charity.

I persuaded M., on whose judgement I depended more than
on my own, to accompany me to the theatre, somewhat against

his inclination, where we saw one of the best plays of my favourite author acted.

By the flattering description given me of Mr. Johnston's powers in such a character as Hamlet, my expectations had been raised to the highest pitch; but I confess they were considerably disappointed. I was far from thinking his performance void of merit. On the contrary, in any passionate dialogue he seemed to excel. His remonstrances with the queen, his mother, were spirited and affecting, as were also some of his railing dialogues with the courtiers. He was master, too, of a certain smile and sometimes a laugh, the most indicative of Hamlet's perturbed state of mind that can be imagined.

At times he gained greatly on the feelings by a sudden depression of his voice, as if shocked by the crowd of dismal ideas recurring to him at once.

These excellencies we must allow him, but he certainly — in many instances — greatly over acted his part: you would lose all patience were I to go through the whole play with him, but do you really think that Shakespeare meant Hamlet to wave his arms, beat his breast, bellow and stamp like a fury in his far fetched reveries? I don't believe it, no more than I believe that Mr. Johnston entered at all times into the spirit of his inimitable author. But there was so much of the play lay on him and he exerted himself so much that, long ere it was done I felt far more for him as Mr. Johnston than as Hamlet.

I thought the Queen and Ophelia well acted, though with regard to the latter some were of a different opinion, pretending that that character had been much better acted by one formerly and that whilst the remembrance of her performance was fresh in the minds of the Edinburgh audience, it was in vain for another to think of appearing in Ophelia to advantage. This was nothing to me and was but bad reasoning in the main.

Mr. Mullender got a good amends of them that night as, Horatio being always in company with Hamlet, they could never hiss him for fear of their darling Mr. Johnston, and Mr. Horatio preached away full well.

But O dear Sir! if ever you have the opportunity, give my compliments to Mr. Rock; that is such a devil of a body as never was born. He acted Polonius in such a manner as confirmed me in my former opinion of his merit in such a character. Shakespeare seems to have intended that Polonius should not understand, or take no notice of, some of Hamlet's retorts — but Mr. Rock understood him well enough and took very good heed to him too. He fixed some looks on him which I neither can forget nor describe; one of them was thus in English, "Gentlemen, if I durst, I would lend you a hearty lounder."

If I read in the Journal that Henry the Fourth was to be acted and Mr. Rock to personate Sir John Falstaff, I would come from Etterick on foot in order to be a spectator. What a terrible

Mr. H. E. JOHNSTON
IN THE CHARACTER OF HAMLET.

figure he would make in a solemn character, such as Cardinal Wolsey. Though it could scarcely be more ridiculous than an Etterick Shepherd prescribing rules to the performers on the Theatre Royal.

Yet he had but three syllables to pronounce in a tragical style that night, which were very far from producing any symptoms of grief; it was when Hamlet stabbed him behind the arras.

"O! I'm slain," said Mr. Rock.

But in such a ludicrous tone that the audience, instead of being shocked at the unhappy mistake, burst out in a roar of laughter; that was all the lamentation they made for Mr. Rock.

"O! I'm slain," said he.

It was like three minums, the first on B, the two last on A.

After Hamlet had thus "compounded him with dust," I did not expect to see any more of him, but was agreeably deceived when he came strutting in as the sexton. As to the propriety of this scene, we shall leave that to Shakespear's commentators, but I never saw any thing acted to the life until I saw the sexton. It is strange that we take more pleasure in a striking imitation of any thing than in the thing itself. I thought if I had seen a sexton digging a grave, whilst he knew not that any saw him, he could scarcely have done any other way than Mr. Rock did — at least if it had come into his head to sing a song; yet I would have been no more delighted with the sight than with any other common occurrence. But when I saw Mr. Rock leaning on his spade and looking this way, and that way, if all was right, then spit on his hands and fall to work; I was so charmed that I was sitting on the waves of the sea — the sexton and all the scenes were moving up and down.

He did not step or leap into the grave but, having plenty of time, he sat down and slid himself in. Here I laughed until I was ashamed!

There was nothing about Hamlet's ghost that could raise the idea of a spirit, saving the chalk upon his face; he brought me in mind of an old raggamuffin, telling his difficulties when a soldier, nor did I ever hear one of them telling their story more like a lie — "Alas poor Yorick."

They acted a sort of bauble afterwards, called the *Purse*, which was neither sense nor nonsense, much as, Sir, you must think these letters of this simple

Shepherd

Sir — *Vanity of vanities, all is vanity.* O Ho! my shepherd is going to commence preacher now, you will say; here, without doubt, follows a sermon. By no means, Sir; but for sundry weighty reasons I have chosen the above text or motto.

For one reason, I am going to write you a Sabbath-day's journal and wished to begin it in a decent manner; and, *2dly,* it furnisheth matter wherewith to begin my letter — a circumstance in which I find more difficulty than in writing all the rest.

I arose early this day and took the road for Queensferry. The morning was fine and all was silence, saving the chirping melody of the birds amongst the woods and hedges; the view was, for the most part, intercepted by thriving plantations and substantial inclosures. I saw enough, however, to convince me of the richness and fertility of the country through which I passed — which is everywhere adorned with gentlemen's seats and seems to be managed according to the most approved modes of cultivation.

In a short time, I arrived at the Royal burgh of Queensferry, most advantageously situated on the southern shore of the Firth, in the midst of a populous country, from which it must derive considerable profit, as well as from its fisheries, coasting trade and the passage of the ferry.

This is a very antient burgh; it is said to have received its charters at an early period and to have been the place where Malcolm Canmore's queen first landed in Scotland — from which circumstance it took its name.

It seems to be a place where there is a considerable stir, a good population and some manufactures. I think the innkeepers on both sides of the ferry should be under proper regulations; the passengers, being obliged to wait time and tide, are so entirely in their power. When I arrived there was no other wanted to pass and, being unwilling to freight a boat, I alighted and ordered my horse a feed of oats. In a very little while, three north country gentlemen came, on their way home from Leith races. I hasted to join them; my horse had not eaten up its corn, yet I had to pay fourpence for hay — at which I was very ill pleased and expostulated with the hostler, but was told that if it had not eaten, it *might* have eaten! This article of forage proved a bone of contention between landlord and me the whole day; but I had more reason to complain before I got back again.

We had a fine passage across the ferry: I was glad to see the rough sailors pay a respect to that holy day. They spoke little and I did not hear an oath minced by one of them.

One young gentleman, being newly come from such variety of entertainments, had forgot — I dare say — that it was the Sabbath, for he placed himself on the stern of the boat and fell a-whistling Greig's Pipes with great glee. The passengers looked at one another and even the boisterous ferry-men laughed in their sleeve. When he understood himself, his looks were amusing, but his pride would not suffer him to acknowledge — even in action — that he was wrong. He left whistling

that tune and tried another, which by degrees died
kept silent the rest of the passage.

In a short time I was at Inverkeithing, a considera
situated on a rising ground at the head of a fine bay or
where they annually ship a prodigious quantity of coa
the construction of the roads and the waggons to suit them, they
drive them to the shore with the greatest facility that I was
astonished at seeing two small horses drag such a quantity.

You would be little edified — and less amused — were I to
describe the crops on every spot that I passed and it is certainly
the greatest arrogance in a stranger pretending to describe a
country from what he sees by the wayside; or to give the
character of the inhabitants from those he accidentally meets or
converses with. It is probable I will err in this respect; from
what I saw and heard I formed my notions and these notions,
though never so absurd, to you I will communicate.

And certainly, various causes have conspired to check the
agricultural improvement in Fifeshire and have kept it longer in
a state of infancy than might have been expected, either from
the soil or numerous population: for the crops were much
inferior to those in the Lothians and, in the higher parts, agriculture seemed quite neglected. The fences were bad and much
of the ground bare and unimproved.

On entering Blair-Adam's lands, however, the face of the
country wore somewhat a better aspect. I met and overtook
great numbers of the inhabitants going to and coming from
church and, although they appeared to advantage — dressed in
their Sunday's clothes, on a fine summer day — I found the
peasantry, especially the fair sex, much inferior to our border-
ers, both in person and features.

The next thing that engaged my attention was Loch-Leven, a
beautiful sheet of water about 12 miles in circumference; I was
curious to learn the derivation of the name and if it meant the
same with Lommond, but could gain no satisfaction. Yet is it
not worthy of remark that the Leven issues out of Loch Lomond
and Loch Leven is bounded by the Lomond hills?

With pleasure I fixed mine eyes on the old castle on one of its
islands, whose name so early and so often occurs in our Scottish
history, which yet I could not help viewing as a standing
memorandum of Scotish baseness as well as Scotish bravery.

There, again and again, have an handful of our brave countrymen maintained themselves against armies of their adversaries,
when the whole country around was in their possession.

There, too, did the intrepid Henry Piercy, son to the Earl of
Northumberland, suffer a tedious captivity after his defeat at
Otterburn.

But, as a counterpoise to these instances of valour in our

◁ North Queensferry

edecessors, there injured and amiable majesty suffered imprisonment, and that by the very persons who were bound by the laws of God and man to reverence and obey her — who have left an indelible blot on their name and nation, who swayed by prejudice and selfish ends made a handle of a few youthful levities natural to her sex and station, to violate the sacred rights of sovereignty; to hunt and persecute their lawful queen; oblige her to become a fugitive in a foreign land; and there, unmoved, saw her proceeded against as a delinquent and, at last — "Fye, fye upon't."

I'll tell you, my dear Sir, religion is a very good thing of itself, but it is dreadful when abused as a mask; and here hath been more evil done under a pretence of religion than anything else — love not excepted. We're oft to blame in this.

"'Tis too much prov'd, that with devotion's visage,
And pious accent we do sugar o'er, The devil himself."
(Hamlet)

Kinross is pleasantly situated at the head of the loch and is a long, cleanly town, but neither so large nor so elegant as our own county town.

"'Tis no great affair then," you will say.

It is the seat of the sheriffs and justice courts and possesseth a good linen manufactory. In McLaren's inn, amongst other things, I got a large Loch Leven trout served up to me — I immediately recognised a great similarity in taste and colour to the Loch-Skene trouts in our neighbourhood. I desired to see some of those which were new taken and the likeness in shape were still more striking! The fishing in the loch is an article of much benefit to Kinross.

Milnathorpe, a little north of it, is a very thriving village and, upon the whole, this small county seems to be fast improving, as many fields are in far better order than others immediately adjoining.

The sheep are now expelled to the ridge of hills that separate it from Stratherne, which are much over-run with furze. Here I saw a large flock of the most handsome little square sheep I ever saw in my life: I suppose they were of the Shetland breed, for I never saw any of the same stamp before. Excepting a few tup lambs at Edinburgh, these were the only sheep I saw betwixt the borders of Tweeddale and Blair in Athol, a distance of about ninety miles.

I now traversed the extensive valley of Stratherne, crossed the river at a bridge, where there is a village and a good inn. The view here was interesting — there the Erne winding down a beautiful and fertile valley, its banks everywhere adorned, both by nature and art; here the Craig of Moncrieff presented its bold and craggy columns to the rays of the sun, reflecting its heat on the valley and shielding it from the biting blasts of the north.

I was quite sick of travelling between two hedges and wished to be amongst hills again, wherever they were. Having been bred amongst mountains I am always unhappy when in a flat country. Whenever the skirts of the horizon come on a level with myself I feel myself quite uneasy and have generally a headache. This was the reason why I flew over the lands of Fife and Kinross like a Hebridean eagle who, from a visit to the banks of Forth, was sailing back to her native cliffs and, on reaching the eminence above the Tay, the objects that would have ravished others were by me quite overlooked.

There, a large river winding between two romantic hills and watering the finest carse of Scotland.

Here, a compact, elegant city, all around adorned by beautiful villas, woods and orchards, while vessels of considerable burden were coming and going on the river.

These scenes would have rivetted the eyes of most travellers, but like the old wooers, I looked too high for them and fixed mine eyes on the lofty mountains which now arose to my view in the head of Angus and the district of Glenshee, specked with the snows of the last century.

I had, alongst with my aged parents, been thrust from our little patrimonial farm and, though possessed of more partiality for my native soil than I am willing at all times to acknowledge, my heart exulted in the thought of finding, amongst the Grampian mountains, a cheap and quiet retreat in the bosom of some sequestered glen where, unawed by the proud, or unenvied by any, I would nourish and increase my fleecy store and awaken, with the pipe and the violin, echoes which had slept for a thousand years, unless aroused to a transient hum by the voice of the hunter, or the savage howl of the wild beast of the desert.

"Vanity of vanities," says the Preacher, "vanity of vanities, all is vanity."

James Hogg

Blair-in-Athol
Monday 26th July 1802

Dear Sir — I know no better way of beginning this letter than by reminding you that I did not make all the observations in my last on the Sabbath day; I have now travelled that road four times and each time saw or heard something new.

I now arrived at the town of Perth, the capital of that extensive county, and was astonished at its magnitude, but more at its elegance and cleanness, considering its low situation.

Although I have traversed its principal streets over and over again, I can make few remarks on it from my own observations, for indeed I had no other method of ascertaining its wealth and

traffic than by reading the sign-boards and examining the goods exhibited in the windows of its shops; nor of its population than by counting the inhabitants by scores, like sheep — and even then I would have been uncertain, as I might have reckoned some twice over!

But as all these were only secondary motives of my journey and as the description of the establishments in and about Perth would be tedious and uninteresting to you, I shall pass on with only observing that I heard of linen, cotton and paper manufactories on extensive scales: of lucrative fisheries and a large traffic both by sea and land; but not a word of a woolen manufactory — I may surely venture to accost them as the lunatic did the priest: "The more fools are they!"

The country in the neighbourhood of Perth bore evident marks of the advantages derived from the vicinity of a large town. For several miles the ground was well cultivated and the crops good. The turnip husbandry indeed is yet in its infancy hereabouts — I often looked for turnips, in vain, for many miles together. For the rearing of this excellent root the banks of the Tay are admirably calculated and what a pity it should not be generally cultivated: the profits arising from its culture are now well ascertained, the crop being lucrative and the soil pulverised and enriched.

Here the farmer could at all times procure lean sheep and cattle from the Highland hills at an easy rate, which he might with small trouble feed off, to sell at an average one-third advanced in price — and for such Perth would furnish at all seasons a ready market; whilst the practice would encourage to a greater degree the rearing of sheep on the adjacent mountains.

The proprietors of the land in this country are much more studious to shelter, adorn and enhance the future value of their estates by plantations than those of the south of the Tweed, which at once shews a disinterested liberality of sentiment. Who can regard with indifference the man who, foregoing present emolument for more enlarged views, drops the acorn in the earth and lays the foundation which shall prove a source of wealth, strength and utility to his country when he is mouldering in the dust?

I now saw some ground laid out in the south-country manner, turnips were cultivated on a large scale and promised to turn out well. I asked the name of the farm and was told that it was Longcarty and managed by Mr. Oliver from the eastern border.

On hearing the name Longcarty, I was desirous of learning if the inhabitants had any remembrance of that memorable battle, handed down to them by tradition; or if any traces of it remained on the ground occupied by the contending armies. Being directed to a retainer on that farm — a very sensible, intelligent young man — he shewed me the only remains of the encampments on two small eminences betwixt the road and the Tay, and which were scarcely recognizable as such. He shewed me the very spot where Hay's cottage stood; the field on which he and his sons were ploughing; and the path where they encountered their flying friends. He described the several incidents of the engagements with accuracy and with a warmth which convinced me that the pride of national independence was not yet obliterated on the minds of the Caledonian youths; and that they are possessed of spirits as capable of being aroused to great noble actions in the persons of free subjects of the British empire, as in those of feudal vassals, all the quarters of the globe can now bear ample testimony.

The spacious St. Laurence hath seen them conquer; the rapid Rhine hath borne attestation to their bravery; and the muddy Nile hath sworn the fact.

I did not in the least expect to have every local circumstance pointed out to me with such precision as was done by that young man, especially when I considered that, of many battles of a much later date fought in the south, no traces remain save in the historic page.

You will readily conclude that the whole of them are purely ideal, and the creation of a fancy equally acquainted with the history and the local situation of the place. I dare not say that this is not the case but, were I to venture an opinion, I would say I rather think them real. Had they been founded on supposition the different places would be more contiguous, nor would the river have been suffered to divide the scene. Although I believe that no event in our annals of so early a date is even pretended to be described with such traditional exactness, yet this may in some measure be accounted for: the narrow escape which Scottish liberty had from being overwhelmed by the waves of foreign oppression made the issue of the day more than ordinary dear unto them, which the constant residence of the family — then ennobled — in those parts would keep up the story pure and unadulterated by romance.

The peasantry on the borders of the Tay and the Erne, through which I passed, are habited in the same manner as those south of the Forth, saving that the broad bonnet is universally worn. They are rather below than above the middle size, stout made, have ruddy healthful countenances and are much more mild and frank in their disposition than the austere Lothianer. They generally enter into matrimony when young and appear to enjoy as much happiness, both social and domestic, as their capacity or their situation can admit of.

I now left Auchtergaven, near which stands a good inn. A little way above it there is a large morass of a great depth, brought under cultivation — which must surely have been done at a considerable expense. I spoke with some of Sir George Stuart's tenants who were driving marl for him, to which they were bound in their tenures as a small remembrance of their ancient state of villainage.

My road now led through Birnam wood, which seems to have grown out of the stumps of that which Malcolm's army cut up and carried to Dunsinnan as it was all, or mostly, quite young. Birnam hill is steep and rugged.

Dunkeld and the scenery around it, quite surpass anything that ever I saw in beauty. It is situated at the head of a fine valley, through which the Tay flows in many serpentine turns and gentle bendings and in the bosom of romantic hills, crowned with wood to the very tops. Its inhabitants will never be sensible from what airth the wind blows, unless they can judge from the clouds flying over their heads.

In short, Sir, you may paint to yourself the most charming landscape that you can conceive; you may unite propriety with elegance; elegance with beauty; and beauty with sublimity; yet you never will match Dunkeld if you have not seen it. To render it a masterpiece, nature and art have combined their efforts. Although I have spent my youth in obscurity, I was yet surprised that the beauty of Dunkeld had never reached my ears, farther than in a stanza of an old song which I continued to sing during the remainder of the day.

"Blair-in-Athol's mine Ritchie,
Blair-in-Athol's mine Ritchie,
And Bonny Dunkeld, where I do dwell,
And these shall a' be thine Ritchie."

But indeed, every step that I advanced betwict this and Blair convinced me how woefully I had been mistaken of the country. I had, last year, from the height south of the bridge of Isla, seen the Tay issuing from between black, barren hills and I expected, in ascending, to see a mere wilderness — instead of which, every opening of the glen shewed me so much more of a paradise!

Large forests of wood, both natural and planted, every where arose in view. All sorts of timber thrive to the utmost in Athol and they are planted with a liberal hand. I wished several times that Dr. Johnson had passed that way. I was particularly pleased with majestic appearance of the weeping birch which, uniting the tallness of the cedar with the straightness of the pine, hangs her beautiful tresses all around her white stem in the most graceful attitude imaginable.

Sure the vegetable creation cannot produce her equal, especially high in Athol where she seems to arrive at the most perfect stature: with such an easy modesty does her small boughs descend and kiss each other, the lowest branches often reaching to the ground, the next these, and so on to the top, while "one blast of the southland wind" causeth the most

graceful sweep through all the wood. I could not help viewing her as the queen of the forest, whose modest deportment all the rest of the trees strove to imitate.

You will be very apt to attribute this to some other cause, namely the fitness of the soil, but no where in Scotland do the trees droop their branches as in Athol. The Pine, the laryx and the willow are all around hung with waving twigs; and even the oak, the monarch of the wood, hangs his hardy, dishevelled locks, in imitation of his fair consort.

The Duke of Athol hath erected a farm-house with all its suitable conveniences, in a fine holm about two miles above Dunkeld, the land around which he manageth after the most liberal plan. This, as an example, hath already had considerable effect on the surrounding country; and besides this, he hath many of them bound in their leases to have one-fifth part of their arable land in clover and rye-grass and another fifth-part of it fallow.

I found that his Grace is beloved by his people in general. I conversed with one who told me that he was one of nineteen farmers who were removed from the Duke's land to make way for one man, who now possessed the whole of what they, with their families, lived happily upon. On expressing my astonishment what could move his Grace to such a proceeding, he replied, ''Ah! Cot pless him, hit pe nane of his doings.''

I passed the hill called King's Seat, which riseth immediately from the river with a steep ascent to the top and hath a very striking appearance. This hill they reckon the march between the Highlands and the Lowlands of Perthshire; yea, so exactly does it separate them, that the family below it talk English and the one above it, Gaelic — which is the prevailing language all beyond it.

Saw the junction of the two rivers, Tay and Tummel, where they seemed much of a size: here there were large quantities of wood thrown out by the floods which had been committed to the mercy of the waters in the forests of Athol and Ranach. I had never yet seen any sheep. I was always enquiring for them and was sometimes told they were beyond such and such hills, but that the extensive plantations had banished them mostly from the banks of the rivers.

I now went through the village of Pitlochie and passed by the beautiful house of Faskaly which, with the surrounding scenery, would form a very fit subject for the pencil. Visited the fall of Tumel, a fine cataract — was surprised to hear that salmon sometimes ascended it: but this was not the only instance which I had as proof of the agility and courage of the Highland salmon, having seen sundry other great falls, some of them higher than this, which they ascended annually in great numbers and which

it would never have entered the heads of *our* salmon to have attempted.

Not far from hence, I went into a little public house, merely in order to obtain some intelligence about this interesting place; and the landlord having but one apartment exclusive of the kitchen, was introduced to some company, of whom — after tasting the usquebae — I began my enquiries with avidity.

My anxiety to gain intelligence of some particulars raised suspicions and my writing of them confirmed these suspicions. In short, from less to more, a disagreeable fracas ensued which, for the sake of some connected with it, I shall pass over in silence.

Suffice it to say, I escaped without receiving any injury either in purse or person, for which I have to thank you! Remembering that I had an unsealed letter of recommendation from you to a respectable character, I produced it with a look of the utmost assurance — which entirely turned the scale of affairs in my favour. Before that this letter occurred to me, I was beginning to be at a loss how to proceed and was two or three times at the point of raising the Tinker's Whistle — which is commonly my last resource; or rather my last effort to keep up a sinking courage when all resources fail.

I would, however, recommend it to all travellers to avoid these whisky houses, unless in cases of necessity: they may sometimes be useful between long stages, or in wild districts where the passengers are few and sometimes weary or benighted, and where no man could afford to pay the licence and keep proper accommodation; but in general they are certainly nuisances; hurtful to the morals and industry of the country people and being often kept by the most lazy and tippling individuals, they are apt to take advantage of a stranger.

If you call for a gill in any of these houses, you are sure to have half-a-mutchkin brought to you, of which the meagre householders greedily partake. If you do not offer them their glasses in regular succession, they take it at their own hands; besides, they commonly made me pay as dear for their whisky as I did at the inns, where everything was comfortable and good.

The next thing that engaged my attention was the famous straits of Killicrankie, a notable pass into the wild highlands. Here, I am told, some strangers have turned back who, perceiving the hills to close before them and, as might well be supposed, no passage over them, imagined they had taken a wrong road and actually returned to Blair.

There is now an excellent road, but before that was made I wonder how they passed any way? Here, too, in the year 1746, a body of auxiliary Germans who were marching north against the rebels, made a full stop, refusing to proceed a step further and expostulated with their leaders on the unreasonableness of carrying them beyond the boundaries of human existence.

On a plain beyond the straits it was, where the famous battle of Killicrankie was fought and where, by the death of Viscount Dundee — better known by the title of Claverhouse — a finishing blow was struck to King James's affairs in Scotland. For although Cameron of Lochiel headed the jacobites for some time, yet the issue of the battle at Cromdale entirely broke and dispirited that party.

I made enquiries concerning the circumstances and position of the armies at Killiecrankie, but could learn nothing that was likely to be depended on, farther than being the grave of Claverhouse.

I cannot exactly describe my feelings to you on being placed on the grave of a man whose name is as familiar to every person about Etterick as Mr. Boston's is, although far from being ever mentioned with the same respect. For in fact, Sir, our old people can talk of fairies, ghosts, mermaids and the de'il! mercy on us Sir! the de'il! with kindling ardour in their eyes, but the name of Claverhouse is never mentioned but with the utmost horror and reproach.

We have many wild local traditions of him about Etterick, the only true one of which is that he cut the massy lids from the leaden coffins in Thirlstane's Aisle, which he converted into bullets, wherewith he peppered the covenanters; that they were so taken by some people is certain, for they are now covered with wood and sunk in the ground. But they tell us that he was in close compact with the devil, from whom he got his horse and we are still shewn some terrible precipices over which he rode with the nimbleness of a fox; and that he was proof against lead is as well believed as that you and I are penetrable.

How often, when a child, have I blessed in my heart the soldier who, at the battle of Killicrankie, seeing his master's affairs going to wreck and that Claverhouse carried all before him, loaded his gun with a few sixpenny pieces — which were all the money that he had in the world — and lodged them in the heart of that bloody persecutor!

Away with such stuff. said I, and peace be to thine ashes! thou art now in the true world and I in the false, but thou wert at least a brave man! zealous for the honour of thy sovereign and steady to the last, in the cause at which thou first espoused; the best principle on which either divine or politician can act! and were I certain that thou didst act according to the dictates of thine own conscience, I should revere thy memory as much as some of the hot-brained zealots, whose blood thou didst shed.

"What conscience dictates to be done
Or warns me not to do;

This teach me more than hell to shun;
That more than heav'n pursue."
Yours for ever,

[signature: James Hogg]

Dear Sir — We must now shift the scene from the most charming landscape to the most bleak sterility, the latter being the predominant appearance all above the plain of Strouan; and ever since passing the bridge of Garry, the ground had continued to ascend with a rapidity I had never before witnessed in the course of a river.

The snow appeared before me at a small distance and sheep were constantly in view, although but in small numbers and thinly scattered. The Garry is a large, turbid stream, boiling and roaring from one rock to another and, for the last fifteen miles, its banks exhibit a scene of the most naked desolation and can create in the mind nothing but ideas dismal and gloomy.

There are no plains on the river's sides, nor is there on all the huge mountains around a single green spot of any extent to be seen, being wholly overgrown with heath to the water's edge and miserably encumbered with loose, rough stones.

In the hollows or flats on the sides of the mountains, here and there a few miserable hamlets present themselves which, though a degree better than those in the more northern districts, yet being the first that encounter the view of the traveller on his way northward have, I dare say, ere now brought to recollection Gray's beautiful stanza:
"Full many a gem of purest ray serene,
The dark unfathom'd caves of ocean bear;
Full many a flower is born to blush unseen,
And waste its sweetness on the desert air."
Many a mind capable of all those noble powers which learning and philosophy can improve is here doomed to take shelter from the rude inclemency of the seasons in the midst of a heap of mud — "in a cottage of clay, whose foundation is in the dust" — and in a few years lies down in peace with his fathers in the land of forgetfullness, alike unknowing and unknown. Lord, what is man!

Arriving at Dalnacardoch, I took up my lodgings for the night and, inviting mine host to take a dram with me, he gave me some hints concerning the rural economy of the country. He informed me that he rented a considerable sheep farm of the Duke of Athol; that it lay on both sides of the Garry; and that he had never removed his sheep on account of the storms, for that they always found as much forage below as carried them in until the weather mended.

I was glad to hear this, for I had computed Dalnacardoch to be no less than 1300 feet above the level of the sea and at the same height in the South of Scotland, the ground is commonly inaccessible for several months in the year: but I next day — on surveying the extent of his farm — computed that he had not above one small sheep for every four acres of land.

I know that you will expect a review of the sheep farming of Athol, but there are many places in the Highlands so much alike in soil and situation, that to treat of them distinctly and severally would require a volume in which a redundancy of repetitions would as repeatedly recur as the letter R does in the above line.

To avoid this, I will first lead you in imagination through every glen and brook that I traced and then give you a synoptical view of the whole, accompanied with some reflections on the most probable means of enhancing the value of the Highland estates.

My landlord, after some encomiums on the goodness of the soil and climate of Ranoch, withdrew on pretence that he must necessarily attend an arrangement of his flocks next morning by the break of day, on the mountain to the east. I engaged him to awaken me that I might accompany him and then began to amuse myself by writing and, now and then, by reading notes on the plaister — with which the room abounded. And many of them were a little to the discredit of the inn.

This made me expect none of the best treatment of Dalnacardoch. In this respect, however, I have the advantage of the most travellers; for never having been accustomed to any dainties, if I get a plate set down to me with a large knife on one side and a fork on the other and anything better than a cog of brose, I think I am served like a prince; nor do I ever agitate the bell, unless to call for a dram or to demand a bill. With the latter I *have* sometimes found fault, but never with the entertainment which here, as well as at all the large inns in the highlands, was very good.

Having finished my solitary supper, I retired to rest, revolving in my mind the occurrences of the preceding day, but especially the affair of the little public house. This, in spite of all my efforts to forget it, was always uppermost; and such strong prepossessions did it raise in my mind against the highlanders, that I began to think myself in danger and to repent somewhat in that dark hour of gloomy ideas that I had left the south alone.

I reasoned thus with myself:

"What profit can I expect from this journey? On the contrary, am I not going to throw away much hard-earned money for neither use nor end? And where is the pleasure? Sure, it is not only *vanity* but *vexation of spirit*. As I am not accountable to any body how far I proceed, would it not be better to return through Ranoch and Breadalbane home again?''

Impressed with these ideas and almost resolved on this plan, I fell asleep; and no sooner were mine eyes closed, than I began to dream. I know you will laugh, but it is but what you have always done at me and my vagaries ever since we became acquainted.

I thought I was sitting in my chamber at Dalnacardoch by a window that looked toward the south and writing to you of mountains and plains of unspeakable grandeur and beauty, when you suddenly entered behind me. I held you out the letter, telling you that was the way you sometimes did with me; but without making me any answer to that purpose, you began to upbraid me for my irresolution and wondered how I could so soon relinquish an enterprise of which I seemed to fond.

I then went over the above arguments with some warmth, which you quite disregarded, and were busy all the while adjusting something about your dress, which was much more magnificent than ever I had before seen it; yea, so *braw* were you that, had it not been for your voice and gait, I could not have recognised you.

No sooner had I finished than you left the room, telling me peremptorily to proceed and depend on your promise that I never should repent it. I take you at your word and shall never more think of returning, until my horse halt in the interior of Ross shire, nor shall I repent. Don't think, my dear Sir, that this is a story; it is just as true as preaching and I have been induced to look to you as my guardian angel, while I am, your humble

Ellwich Shepherd

Dalnacardoch
Wednesday 28th July

Dear Sir — I arose early next morning with the sun and enquired for Mr. Robertson, who had gone away to the mountains long before and could not think of awakening me so early. As the investigation of countries such as this was the only errand I had in the Highlands, I ordered breakfast to be got ready and resolved to follow him. In the meantime I sauntered about and looked at his cattle.

Observing a little stout broad fellow building peats, I went up to him and enquired if he staid at the inn. He said he did so at times.

I desired him to accompany me to the top of a little hill which I pointed out; this he did with the greatest readiness; told me the names of such places as were in view; and led me to see a huge log of wood that had been dug out of a moss. I then engaged him to accompany me a day's journey to the westward, where he said we would see the greatest number of sheep and, as soon as we got breakfast, we set off.

John having a small flask of whisky in his pocket, a piece of cold beef, a kebbuck heel and some thin oat-meal cakes rolled neatly up in a cloth, we dreaded neither thirst nor hunger and agreed to turn back when we tired. We passed over the Garry, went across some black moorish hills, the soil of which was much better than it appeared at a distance. Nothing singular occurred for a long while; we made appropriate and infallible remarks on the sheep and the soil; threw stones at plovers and chafed the ptarmigan, which fled fluttering and squeaking to wile us away from her young; until after passing a corry, as John called it, we came to the top of a bank from whence we had a fine view of all the upper parts of Loch Rannoch with the surrounding scenery.

The banks of this loch and the glens around it form the districts of Ranoch, a country that I had always viewed on the map as a remote wilderness, it being the north-west corner of Perthshire and the uttermost of all the branches of the Tay. Yet, on the contrary, it is a very fine highland district, populous and richly adorned with gentlemen's seats.

At the mouths and in opening of the glens, through which the superfluous waters are carried to the loch, there are scenes of inexpressible beauty: the sheep and cattle are excellent and the soil on the sides of the Errochty and the Gaur, strong and grassy. The fuel is abundant, nor are any of the necessaries of life wanting. It is likewise of fine sporting country, either for fishing or fowling; they catch trouts in Loch Ranoch of a prodigious size; some of them are said to weigh above one stone Troy weight. In short, there seems to be fewer inconveniences peculiar to this than almost any other country so far removed from commerce and markets.

It being so well sheltered all around, especially on the north and east, by ranges of high mountains and being of itself rather flat and low-lying, it enjoys a more mild and temperate climate than any other country of the same height in Scotland. The winter storms — I am certainly informed — are never destructive and seldom severe or of long duration. The scenery is a mixture of the beautiful and the sublime, although less of the latter is intermixed than in most highland views; yet, as a contrast to the fine openings and beautiful villas on the west and north of the loch, over against us the *skeleton* of the black forest reminded us of what it once had been; above which the mountain of Schehallion rose to the height of 3587 feet above the level of the sea. This mountain is famous for the experiments made on it by some of the most noted philosophers to ascertain the powers of attraction and gravity.

We now shaped our course northward, traversing a large tract of country, and at length landed on the confines of Loch Erocht, through which we met with little that comes within the compass of this letter. We went into the people's houses with the assurance of village cats, whose grave deportment I was for the most part forced to imitate; for although many of them could talk English, neither my guide nor they ever put it in practice, unless in answering an occasional question — a circumstance not much in favour of their good breeding!

This country must have made very rapid advances in civilisation; it is not yet 60 years since it was noted as a nest of robbers and free-booters, who laid the whole country under contribution as far as the Aila and the Erne: prior to the year 1746, a regiment of soldiers was scarcely sufficient to have brought a thief from Ranoch, but the natives are now as docile and intelligent as any of their neighbours — if not more so.

Many of the young people descending annually into the low country, return with their minds enlightened in rural affairs and their manners more polished, though perhaps not more innocent than when they left their native glens; it is thus that almost every family has become acquainted with the English language.

About three o'clock afternoon, we reached the top of a high hill on the south-east side of Loch Erocht, where we sat down to contemplate an extensive scene of the most savage wildness that the fancy can conceive. A scene which hardly one out of a hundred Scotsmen could even have imagined he should have seen in his own country, on the last week of July; indeed it looked much more like the last of January. I had hitherto been able to count the wreaths of snow that were in my view, but as the upper stories of Ben-Arlenich came in sight, one half of its surface was yet adorned with the massy badges of winter that eternally load its shoulders; each gap was crammed brim full of it, "by its own weight made steadfast and immoveable," and nearly as hard as the rocks which here and there peeped from its surface. It was in many places grown grey with age, or rather by being intermixed with the soil which had been torn from the bleak brows of the mountain. This is one of the most stupendous of those huge masses of deformity that stud the Grampian desart and rises about 4000 feet above the sea.

I insisted on pronouncing it Ben-Erocht, as being synonimous with the lake and river, but John would in nowise hear of it: it rises in the very crown of the country and near the point where the four districts of Athol, Badenoch, Lochaber and Ranoch meet; I think John said that three of these meet on its top.

This mountain interrupted our view northward; the others which we saw around Loch Laggan were in the same state and form. Westward, saving a deep chasm or two that led into the valley of Glencoe, the country was one waste uninhabitable moor, which at that season — and then only — was frequented by the shepherd and his flocks.

The Ochils and the Bens of Breadalbane terminated the view southward; and eastward it was lost and bewildered amongst the vast range of hoary headed Alps, which run in large chains through those trackless forests that surround the utmost limits of the Bruar and sources of the Dee. These, every time the fatigued eye wanders through them, remind one exactly of the billows of the ocean; such a prodigious extent of country is crouded with them, rising and swelling behind one another, and that which the eye fixeth on always appears the largest. The soil being entirely wafted away from their weather-beaten tops and the stones having acquired a whitish scurf, they every one appear besprinkled with silver, or powdered with a "Grimin' of a new fa'n snaw."

I never in my life partook of a dinner with more heartfelt satisfaction than on the bare turf of the summit of this hill. John and I conversed freely on such subjects as chance produced and, though we had no great flow of wit, we laughed most heartily at such as we had. I remember little that passed either here or on our way back to Dalnacardoch, which we reached at a late hour, weary and fatigued. We had, for the sake of the view, placed ourselves at dinner quite out of reach of any means of allaying our thirst, save what the whisky flask afforded, the frequency of our visits to which entirely disarranged the remarks, both sentimental and philosophical, of

Your most affectionate

James Hogg

1803

Dear Sir,—As you were, or pretend to be, much diverted with my whimsical account of a journey which I made through the North Highlands last year, you will not be pleased at hearing that I am now embarked on a long circuit through the Western Highlands and Isles, of which I also intend giving you an account by letters. But in the meantime I promise, nay I swear, that I will endeavour, by making no digressions, and curtailing my remarks to confine this correspondence within more circumscribed bounds than of last year, of which I now proceed to give you an instance.

On the twenty-seventh of May I again dressed myself in black, put one shirt, and two neckcloths in my pocket; took a staff in my hand, and a shepherd's plaid about me, and left Ettrick on foot, with a view of traversing the West Highlands, at at least as far as the Isle of Skye. I took the road by Peebles for Edinburgh, and after being furnished with letters of introduction to such gentlemen as were most likely to furnish me with the intelligence which I wanted respecting the state of the country, I took passage in the 'Stirling Fly' for that town. I got only a short and superficial view of the old palace of Linlithgow, and satisfied myself with only making my uncle's observation on viewing the Abbey of Melrose; 'Our masons can mak nae sic houses now-a-days.'

I got a deal of information as we passed along from the Rev. Mr. Somerville of Stirling, who was a passenger in the coach, and seemed a very specious, intelligent man. He showed me the Earl of Stair's very extensive plan of the battle of Dettingen, and entertained me with many curious remarks respecting the ancient harbour and town of Camella, the capital of the Picts, situated beyond Linlithgow, as also the most minute and just description of the battles of Falkirk and Bannockburn, all of which I have written in my journal, and as they are much better described elsewhere than I am capable of doing, I entirely decline it, though I wish from my heart that the distinctions of Englishmen and Scot were entirely disannulled and sunk in that of Britons. I will tell you a story which was told by one in the coach.

'A good many years ago a North and South Briton fell into a warm dispute about the privileges resulting to each country from the Union; each of them divesting his own country entirely of any share of them. At length the Scot safely observed, that if

the English had no advantage by the Union, why were they so forward in promoting it, and why were the Scots so backward to agree to it?

'Why sir, as to the former, because it freed them from the devastations committed by their plunderings parties. And as to the latter, because it deprived them of the rich booties which they reaved from England at the expiration of every temporary truce.'

'Aye, aye, was that the way? I did not know, I'm unacquainted with history, but what the d——l had the English ado but to wear them back.'

'Why sir, at a fair engagement, in open war they never could stand us; but having their own mountains and forests so near for a safe retreat, it was impossible to prevent their plundering parties from committing frequent depredations.'

'Aye, aye, I did not know these things,' said the Scot, 'and were the English too hard for them at a fair engagement?'

'Indeed sir, they were. The best and bravest of the Scots allowed of that.'

'Aye, aye, I'm unacquainted with history, but it is believed to have been otherwise where I live.'

'Where,' said the Englishman, 'do you live?'

'At Bannockburn!'

'Hem—.'

Not another word ensued. The subject entirely dropped, and the shrewd Caledonian sat squirting in the fire as if he had meant nothing by the answer.'

I lodged on the Castle-hill, in company with a Mr. MacMillan, who came with us in the coach from Edinburgh, and was bound for Lochaber. We arose next morning before the sun, and had a most advantageous and enchanting view of the links of Forth, and the surrounding country, forming altogether a landscape unequalled by any of the same nature in Scotland.

This having been always the principal pass for an army, either to or from the North, hath in consequence been the scene of many bloody encounters. A description of all the battles that have been fought in view of Stirling Castle would furnish matter for volumes. Many of these have been decisive, and settled the fates of thousands, from which dismal circumstance so often occurring, the place in ancient times took the name of Strevlin, or the valley of strife.

We took the road by Doune, and reached Callander of Menteith at eight a.m., where we breakfasted at an inn in company with the laird of Macnab, and after I had furnished myself with some provisions for the day, departed. The management of the land under tillage continued to grow worse, and in the neighbourhood of Callander there were some of it in a very poor and weedy state, which is the more to be regretted as it appears by some fields adjoining that there was the means of enriching it within reach. I did not stay at any of these *towns* to make enquiries into the present state of their population, trade, and manufactures, sufficient to justify an attempt toward a description of them, therefore I will not detain you by a random, or borrowed account of them, but hasten on, lest I break my oath at the very first.

At Kilmahog, a paltry village about a mile beyond Callander, I parted with MacMillan, and crossing the Teith, turning to the left. You may guess that I was glad at getting safely past this village, for its name signifies *the burial place of Hogg*. It is pleasantly situated on the north-east bank of the river, and is intersected by a dam, over which have been erected several buildings. I proceeded several miles without meeting with anything remarkable. I went quite out of my road to see Glenfinlas, merely because it was the scene of a poem in which I delighted, but could see nothing more than in other places. The hills were covered with mist down to the middle; yet I saw enough to convince me that it was an excellent sheep range. Returning, I went by the bridge of Turk, passing a little curiously shaped hill covered with wood, which, with the shores of Loch Venachar, are worthy of going a good way to view even although the Trossachs were not beyond them. But the description of these I must defer until my next, and shall close this as soon as I have reminded you that I have now come above an hundred miles, which would have been four letters at least, last year.

I remain, Sir, your ever faithful

James Hogg

Glen Gyle
Sunday 29th May

Dear Sir, — As I know that you have seen the Trossachs yourself, and as so many have seen them, and no doubt have described them minutely, I will not attempt a particular description of them, but they are indeed the most confused piece of Nature's workmanship that I ever saw, consisting of a thousand little ragged eminences all overhung with bushes, intersected with interstices, the most intricate and winding imaginable.

On entering among them, surely said I, mentally, Nature hath thrown these together in a rage. But on seeing the spreading bushes overhanging the rocks, and hearing the melody of the birds, I softened the idea into *one of her whims*. But as I had set out with a mind so intent on viewing the scenery of the Highlands, and coming to such an interesting place on the very first

48

day that I entered them, I was more than ordinarily delighted. It was a little past noon on a Sabbath day when I arrived there. The air was unusually still and dark, not a breath moved the leaves that hung floating over the impending precipes of the Trossachs, nor caused one dark furl on the smooth glassy surface of the winding Loch Katrine. Every species of the winged creation that frequent the woods and mountains of Caledonia, were here joined that day in a grateful hymn in praise of their great Creator. Not one key remained untouched of all the Italian gamut. It was indeed a Dutch concert, where everyone sung his own song, from the small whistle of the wren, to the solemn notes of the cuckoo, sounded on an E and C, a double octave lower, and from the sprightly pipe of the thrush and blackbird, to the rough harp of the pye and raven. And that the anthem might be complete, the imperial eagle hovered like a black mote in the skirts of the mist, at whose triumphant yell all the woodland choristers were for some seconds mute; and like menials in the presence of their lord, began again one after another with seeming fear and caution.

The landscape at large was quite spoiled by a thick, lowering mist, that hid in shades all the high mountains which should have made up the back-ground of this romantic scene. It also confined, and bowed down my contemplations to what most

49

employs them, namely, the things below. These, on such a day, would naturally have arisen, with my eyes, to the tops of the hills, and from thence to heaven, and consequently to Him who made heaven and earth and — the Trossachs. But knowing, notwithstanding of our mental depravity, that clouds and darkness surround Him, and as I was become surrounded with mist, I knew it needless even to attempt it. I had no guide along with me, and it is probable that I might miss some of the most interesting places. I lost myself in the mazes of the river, and for a while believed, what was impossible, namely, that I had got to the other side of the river without perceiving it. The manner in which it works its way amongst the rocks, is not the least striking of the whole. One while it seems quite impeded in its progress, at other times, wheeling and boiling in the most terrific manner, always in ferment, and in a seeming perplexity at what chasm it shall next make its escape by.

I took my dinner, consisting of some biscuits and a cut of cheese, beside a crystal spring at the foot of a rock; and during my stay there had formed a definite conclusion respecting the formation of the Trossachs. I concluded, that prior to the universal deluge, the Trossachs had formed a steep bar between the two hills, and that the whole of Glen Gyle and Loch Katrine had been one loch, which had formed subterraneous passages among the rocks, to such an extent as had prevented it filling up; but on the declension of the waters of the Flood from around it, unable to sustain the mighty pressure, the Trossachs had given way; when the impetuous torrent had carried all before it saving the everlasting rocks, which yet remain, the shattered monuments of that dreadful breach. This theory is supported by two remaining evidences. First, that the western side of these eminences are all bare and solid rock; while on the opposite sides of the larger ones there are quantities of loose stones and some soil amassed. And second, that the ravines are deeper, and the knolls higher, on, and near, the bottom of the glen, and continue gradually to diminish as you ascend the hills on each side, until they totally disappear. However, my dear sir, I have no hopes that you will treat this probable discovery with a greater share of approbation than you do all my natural and experimental philosophy, namely, by laughing at it.

I now left the Trossachs, and proceeded up the north side of loch Katrine, on the shores of which there is still a good proportion of wood, though small in comparison with what it seems once to have been. Many extensive banks that have once been covered with large trees, are only recognizable to have been so by thousands of decaying stumps. Even the Trossachs themselves have suffered severely in wild beauty by the ravages of the axe. But what they have lost in beauty they have gained in

◁ Loch Katrine

utility. They are now covered with stocks of tolerably good sheep, and there is still a sufficiency of wood to serve them for shelter in winter, which is all that is requisite for the store farmer. The lands belong mostly, either to the Hon. Miss Drummond, or the Earl of Moray, and are generally, though not very large, good sure farms, and will in time bring large rents.

The inhabitants acknowledge that they do not suffer by snows lying long in winter, but that, owing to the dryness of their herbage, their flocks are often much reduced in condition during the spring months, and that when the lambing season commences with them, many of the lambs are in danger of perishing.

I began now to be afraid that I might be disappointed of a lodging during the night, there being no public houses in the bounds. I went on, however, without asking, until I came to the house of Glen Gyle. It was then growing late, and there was no human habitation for many miles. I had, twelve years ago, been sent on an errand to the house of Glen Gyle, to ask permission of McGregor, the laird, to go through his land with a drove of sheep. He was then an old man, and seemed to me to be a very queer man; but his lady granted my request without hesitation, and seemed to me an active, social woman. Therefore I expected, from the idea that I had formed of her character, to be very welcome there, and never knew, until I went to the house, that the laird was dead, and the lady and her family removed to the neighbourhood of Callander; while the farm and mansion-house were possessed by two farmers. When I called, one of them came to the door. I asked the favour of a night's lodging; but the important McFarlane made use of that decisive moment to ask me half a score of questions before he desired me to walk in. I experienced the greatest kindness and attention from all the family when once I got amongst them. McAlpin the other farmer, I found to be a very considerable man, both in abilities and influence, but the most warm and violent man in a dispute, though ever so trivial, that ever entered into one. If any one advanced a theory of which he did not approve, he interrupted them with a loud and passionate *hububub*. On the preceding summer five gentlemen from Glasgow were benighted there, and calling at the door, desired McAlpine to speak with them. He sent word that they might go about their business, for he would be d —— d if he held any conversation with a pack of Glasgow weavers.

I remain yours, etc.,

James Hogg

52

Dear Sir, — There is nothing about Glen-Gyle that admits of particular description. It is situated at the head of Loch Katrine, and surrounded by Black rocks. It was one of Rob Roy's principal haunts, to whom Glen-Gyle was related. McAlpin showed me the island in Loch Katrine where he confined the Marquis of Montrose's steward, after robbing him of his master's rents, and where he had nearly famished him. The McGregors have a burial place at Glen-Gyle, surrounded by a high wall. On one of their monuments their coat of arms and motto are engraved. Query. Was it not remarkable that both you and I should, each of us have made Glen-Gyle a party in a ballad in imitation of the ancients, and that before we had either seen or heard of each other? Answer. The poetical sound of the name, Sir.

I now left Glen-Gyle in order to cross the mountains into Glenfalloch. I did not, however, take the nearest way, but held towards the top of the hill on the left hand, from which I knew there was a charming prospect, with which I had formerly been greatly surprised. As I hinted before, I had in the summer of 1791 passed through that country with sheep. On a Saturday night we lay with our sheep in the opening of a wood by the side of Loch Ard, and during the whole of the Sabbath following there was so dark a fog, that we could scarcely see over our drove. Although we got permission, we did not go by Glen-Gyle, but by the garrison of Inversnaid, and the night again overtook us on the top of this hill. The mist still continued dark, and though my neighbour (companion,) who was a highlandman, knew the road, I was quite unconscious what sort of a country we were in. When I waked next morning the sun was up, and all was clear, the mist being wholly gone. You can better judge of my astonishment than I can express it, as you are well aware what impression such a scene hath on my mind. Indeed it was scarcely possible to have placed me in another situation in Scotland where I could have had a view of as many striking and sublime objects by looking about me. Loch Katrine with its surrounding scenery stretching from one hand; Loch Lomond on the other. The outline of Ben Lomond appeared to particular advantage, as did the cluster of monstrous pyramids on the other side. One hill, in the heights of Strathfillan, called Ben Leo, was belted with snow, and from that direction had a particularly sharp, peaked appearance, being of a prodigious height.

Besides all this I had drank some whisky the preceding evening, and had a very indistinct recollection of our approach to that place, and it was actually a good while ere I was persuaded that everything I saw was real. I sat about an hour contemplating the different scenes with the greatest pleasure,

before I awakened my comrade.

I was very anxious to be on the same spot again, and went out of my way to reach it, expecting to experience the same delightful feelings that I had done formerly. In this, however, I was disappointed, but was not a little surprised on recollecting the extraordinary recurrence of circumstances as to time and place. It was not only the same day of the week but the same day of the same month when I was on the same spot before. The two Sabbaths preceding these two days had been as remarkable for mist and darkness, in short, my whimsical fortune seemed endeavouring to make me forget the twelve years that had elapsed. But it would not do.

Musing on these objects I fell into a sound sleep, out of which I was at length awakened by a hideous, yelling noise. I listened for some time before I ventured to look up, and on throwing the plaid off my face, what was it but four huge eagles hovering over me in a circle at a short distance; and at times joining all their voices in one unconceivable bleat. I desired them to keep at a due distance, like Sundhope's man, for I was not yet dead, which, If I had been, I saw they were resolved that I should not long remain a nuisance amongst the rocks of Glenfalloch.

I now shaped my course towards Kieletur, on the head of the glen, possessed by Mr. Grieve, from the south country, intending to reach Glenorchy that night, for I supposed that I had a cousin, a shepherd, there, whom I had not seen for twelve years, and whom I esteemed very much. But before I reached Kieletur I learned that Mr. Grieve was absent at the fair on Dumbarton Muir, and that my cousin had left Glenorchy, and was gone to a shealing at the back of Ben Vorlich, where he was herding for Mr. Wallace of Inverouglas. I then turned back, took my dinner at the change-house of Glenfalloch, and going through the hills, reached my friend's hut that night.

This Glenfalloch which I now left is the property of Mr. Campbell. It is divided into large farms, and having been long under sheep the hills are become green, and the stocks very good. My cousin's cottage is situated by a small lake called Loch Sloy, in as savage a scene as can be conceived, betwixt the high, rugged mountains and Ben Vorlich and Ben Vane. The brows of each of these were adorned with old wreaths of snow, and though it was near the month of June so much snow fell during the night that I was there that the heat of the next day did not nearly dissolve it on the tops of these hills. He received me with all the warmth of the most tender friendship, lamenting that he could so ill accommodate me. I soon made him easy on that score, and then he was never satisfied in his enquiries about the welfare of his dearest relations and friends in Ettrick. The family consisted of eleven in all that night, and indeed we

◁ Loch Lomond from Inveruglas

were curiously lodged. They were but lately come to that place, and had got no furniture to it; nor indeed was it any wonder, it being scarcely possible to reach it on foot. We slept on the same floor with four or five cows, and as many dogs, the hens preferring the joists above us. During the night the cattle broke loose, if they were at all bound, and came snuffing and smelling about our couch, which terrified me exceedingly, there being no rampart nor partition to guard us from their inroads. At length I heard, by the growling of the dogs, that they were growing jealous of them. This induced me to give them the hint, which they were not backward in taking, for they immediately attacked their horned adversaries with great spirit and vociferation, obliging them to make a sudden retreat to their stalls, and so proud were the staunch curs of this victory gained in defence of their masters, that they kept them at bay for the rest of the night. Had it not been for this experiment, they could scarcely have missed tramping to death some of the children, who were lying scattered on the floor. Add to all this confusion, that there was an old woman taken very ill before day. We were afraid of immediate death, and Walter Bigger, the other shepherd, manifested great concern, as not knowing how it was possible to get her to a Christian burial-place. Should she die, I think they will be obliged to bury her where they are.

Now sir, mark this situation, and join me in admiring my whimsical fortune, which seems to take a pleasure in reverses, by thus carrying me out of one extremity into another. I say, mark my company here in this hovel. I was in the midst of dying wives, crying children, pushing cows, and fighting dogs; and this very next day, at the same hour, in the same robes, same body, same spirit, I shall be in the splendid dining-room in the Castle of Inverary, surrounded by dukes! lords! ladies! silver, silk, gold, pictures, powdered lacqueys, and the devil knows what! O Mr. Scott, Mr. Scott, thou wilt put me stark mad some day.

Now I say, is it a light? Was it showing any regard for a poor bard's brains, knowing as you well do how susceptible his mind is of impressions corresponding with the different images conveyed by his senses, to persuade him to go through the Trossachs, and the Duke of Argyll's bowling-green, than which no scenery can be more creative than ideas, although sublime, yet gloomy and severe; and as a contrast to thrust me all at once, out of these, headlong amidst all the transcendent beauty, elegance, and splendour of Inveraray. Well, you think nothing of this, but if I lose my judgement, what have you to answer for?

I remain, dear Sir, your most obliged

Ettrick Shepherd

Inverary Castle
Wednesday 1st June

Dear Sir, — It would be by far too tedious were I to give you a minute detail of all my proceedings about Inverary; yet it would be unpardonable were I to omit describing some of my principal blunders and embarrassments; for every hour since the time that I arrived here was marked by one or other of these.

I sent a man from the inn with your letter to Colonel Campbell, who returned his compliments, naming the hour when *he would do himself the pleasure of waiting on me!* Mark that, sir. He was punctual to his time; and immediately took me with him to the Castle. His unaffected simplicity of manners soon rendered me quite easy and happy in his company. He led me through a number of the gayest apartments, and at length told me he was going to introduce me to Lady Charlotte. 'By no means,' said I, 'for heaven's sake. I would be extremely glad could I see her at a little distance, but you need never think that I will go in amongst them.' 'Distance!' exclaimed he. You shall dine with her to-day and to-morrow.' So saying he went towards a door. I declare, the idea of being introduced to a lady of whom I had heard so much as a paragon of beauty, elegance, and refined taste; and who had been the grace and envy of

Courts, raised in my breast such a flutter, I cannot tell you how I felt. He then bolted into a small circular room in one of the turrets, where her ladyship was sitting with some others, closely engaged in something but I cannot tell what it was were I to die for it: and I am vexed to this hour that I had not noted what they were employed in when alone.

She stood up and received me with the greatest familiarity and good humour in the world, which she hath entirely at command; told me the other ladies' names, and enquired kindly for you and Mrs. Scott; then asked some questions about Ettrick Banks and Yarrow Braes. All which I answered in the best manner I was able. I saw that by her assumed vivacity she was endeavouring to make me quite easy; but it was impossible. I was struck with a sense of inferiority, and was quite bamboozled. I would never have known that I was so ill had there not unluckily been a mirror placed up by my leg. Not knowing very well where to look, I looked into it. Had you seen the figure I made, you would have behaved just as I did. My upper lip was curled up, my jaws were fallen down, my cheeks were all drawn up about my eyes, which made the latter appear very little, my face was extraordinary red, and my nose seemed a weight on it. On being caught in this dilemma I really could not contain myself, but burst out a-laughing. The ladies looked at one another, thinking I was laughing at them. However, to bring myself off, I repeated something that the Colonel was saying, and pretended to be laughing at it. I should soon have been as ill as ever I was, had not he relieved me by proposing to withdraw in order to see some paintings which we were talking of. Her ladyship, however, thought proper to accompany us through several apartments, leading her little daughter by the hand, a most beautiful stem of the noble bough.

On coming to the north door of the castle the Colonel ordered a man to play upon a pipe which was concealed in a walking cane of his, and which sounded exactly like the bagpipe at a distance. When the Duchess came within hearing of the music she danced round, setting to the sweet little child, and when she thought that Jack, as she called him, was too severe in his jokes upon Sir William Hart, she popped his hat over the rail, into the sunk way. I was extremely gratified by this behaviour of her ladyship, it became her so well, and I was certain that it was assumed, merely on account of seeing me at such a loss.

Now you will be expecting that I should still be in a worse condition when first introduced to his Grace the Duke, and indeed I was within a little way of being very ill, but got off better than could have been expected. This plaguey bluntness! shall I never get rid of it? He was much indisposed, and I did not see him all day, but he sent in his compliments with Colonel Campbell, desiring to see me at dinner with him tomorrow. The first time that we encountered was thus. I was returned from the top of Duniqueich, and just as I reached the castle gate, a coach drove up, out of which an old gentleman with a cocked hat, and a scarlet coat alighted. I thought him some old officer, and mounted the steps without minding him, but meeting on the flags Captain Campbell, with whom I had been in company before I asked who these were. He said they were the Duke and Doctor Campbell. He was by this time advancing toward me, and I was not knowing how I should address him. But he, who it seems had been enquiring who I was, relieved me by addressing me by name, and welcoming me to Inveraray. I thanked his Grace, and hoped he was got better of his indisposition. He said he was rather poorly yet, and desired me to walk in: adding, 'your friend Colonel Campbell will be here immediately.' I followed his Grace through the dining-room, where he had the condescension to sit down and hold a few minutes tête-a-tête with me. He said I had arrived in a very good season for getting a peaceable and undisturbed view of Inveraray, and asked if I had yet been shown anything that was worthy of notice. I said the Colonel had taken such pains in showing me both the inside of the castle and the policies around it. 'Then,' said he, smiling, 'I am sure that you have seen more than you are pleased with, and that you are even more pleased than edified.' I assured his Grace that I considered myself not a little instructed, as well as pleased, by having seen so much that was quite unequalled by anything that I had ever seen before. He at length desired me to amuse myself with with these books and charts, for that he must go and dress. I had not sat long when Colonel Campbell entered, who in a little time left me also, on the same pretence, that of *dressing for dinner*. I said he was well enough dressed; it was a silly thing that they could not put on clothes in the morning that would serve them during the day. He proved that that would never do, and went his way laughing.

It was not long until the Duke rejoined me, all clad in black, as indeed all the gentlemen were who sat at table. I was always in the utmost perplexities, not knowing servants from masters. There were such numbers of them, and so superbly dressed, that I daresay I made my best bow to several of them. I remember in particular of having newly taken my seat at dinner, and observing one behind me I thought he was a gentleman wanting a seat, and offered him mine.

I was proud that although I did not know how to apply one third of the things that were at table, unless I called for a thing I would not take it when offered to me. I had called for a shave of beef, and was falling on without minding either gravy, mustard, or spice, which were proffered. I refused all. 'What!' said the Colonel, 'L—d do ye eat your beef quite plain?' 'Perfectly plain, sir,' said I, 'saving a little salt, and so would you if you knew how much more wholesome it were.' By great good fortune I was joined by several in this asseveration which my extremity suggested.

The Duke talked freely to me about his farming, and told me he had given orders to Mr. ——, who had the superintendence of all his rural affairs, and who was a very sensible man, and a countryman of my own, to take a ride with me tomorrow and show me his cattle, sheep, etc. I shall give you an account of our ride in my next, until when

I remain, Sir, with the utmost respect, yours,

James Hogg

Dear Sir, — You must now suppose me mounted on a fine brown mare, as light as the wind, and as mad as the devil, and Mr. —— on an excellent grey pony, riding full drive through part of the Duke's land which he occupied himself. We took a view of his breeding cows and some oxen, which were greatly superior to any that I ever saw in beauty and compactness. They are certainly the best breed of Highland cattle produced in Scotland, and indeed they have advantages which it is beyond the power of most men to afford. I have been told that Campbell of Islay, and he only hath long disputed the field with Argyll for the best breed of Highland cattle, and it is the opinion of some that although the latter frequently outsells the other at the markets, yet it is as much owing to the great distance that the Islay cattle must needs be driven, as to the superiority of the breed. It is truly amazing the prices that these two houses draw for their cattle, it being much more than double the average price at Dumbarton Market.

The sheep that we saw were partly of the Cheviot, and partly of the Scotch kinds; but both rather of inferior breed. Mr.—— excused this by alleging that the Cheviot breed was but lately introduced, and they had not had time to improve them, and that the other kind was got from some of the Duke's farmers who were removing, and who could not otherwise dispose of them at value. However it was, they were on excellent pasture that would have produced the best of sheep; and I remarked to Mr. —— that it was a shame to see such a stock upon such land. He was not better pleased with many of my observations, than I was with him in general.

On our return his grace asked me several things, and amongst others, what I thought of Mr. ——. I said I did not rightly understand him; he was surely the worse of drink. 'That was impossible,' he said, 'at this time of day;' and besides, said he, 'I conversed with him since your return. He is perfectly sober. You surely must be mistaken about Mr. ——.' 'I certainly am mistaken my lord,' said I, 'for I look on him as the worst specimen of your Grace's possessions that I have seen about all Inveraray.' Perhaps I said too much, but I could not help telling my mind. Colonel Campbell was like to burst during this dialogue, and indeed, little as he pretended to know about rural economy, I could have gathered more from a three hours' conversation with him, than I could have done with Mr. —— in as many weeks. His whole consisted in boasting.

His Grace had the kindness that day to walk with me up to the workshops where his mechanics were employed, and showed and described to me, several specimens of curious implements in husbandry, too tedious here to describe, many of which were of his own contrivance. He takes a visible pleasure in the study of agriculture, and in rural improvements, of which the valley of Glen Shira is a convincing proof. How creditable a pursuit this, compared with those which many of our inferior nobility delight themselves in! And how happy is the county of Argyll in having such a man placed in the middle of it, whose inclination to do good is as ample as his power of doing it! His venerable age, the sweetness and simplicity of his manners, with the cheerful alacrity showed by every one of the family to his easy commands are really delightful. He is indeed, in the fullest sense of the word, a father to his country. The numerous tenants on his extensive estates, both on the mainland and in the isles, are all gentlemen, even those of the smallest kind are easy in circumstances, happy in their families, and have an implicit confidence in the integrity of their illustrious chief, and every one of them, I daresay in cases of urgency would follow him or Lorne to the field, nor will it be every foe that will keep it, *when the Campbells are coming.*

I had heard it abroad that a man's disposition was best known by the characters of the people whom he had chosen to act under him; I was happy to find that here they were not all Mr. ——. There is a Colonel Graham, whom I was only a few minutes in company with at the village, in whom the Duke placeth an unlimited confidence; and he hath the character of being every way worthy of it. He is strictly a very superior man in every respect.

I am truly ashamed of the attention paid to my by Colonel Campbell. He is indefatigable in his endeavour to make me understand the use and the meaning of every thing, both within and without the castle, made his sister again and again play upon the organ, because I admired it; led me through the whole castle to the very battlements; through every walk of the gardens; every corner of the large barns; and all the office houses; to the very dog-kennel; and made me give names of two young dogs, which I called Suwarrow and Lion. It is a question if ever they were more minded; but this reminds me of an anec-

dote which I shall here relate. 'How is that young dog of mine so much leaner than the others? said Colonel Campbell to the keeper. "I don't know," said he. "You don't know! But you ought to be better to mine." "No," said he pertly, "I will be as good to Mr. Robert's as to yours." "Aye," said the Colonel, "but you act like a puppy in being better to any man's dogs than your master's." The lad looked this way and that way; patted the dog on the head, and had no answer. When the other saw that, he gave him half a crown for being so good to his brother's dog. Colonel Campbell also walked many miles through the woods and fields with me, in order to give me the most advantageous views of the different scenery surrounding that celebrated place, until he was sometimes extremely warm, and he would not suffer me to turn my eyes that way until he came to certain places in order that the view might burst on me all at once, and which he believed to be greatly assisting in the effect it produced.

When he wished that the environs of Loch Dow and Glen Shira should open to me all at once, that I might not see it by halves as we advanced, he placed his huge bulk on that side of me, laid his arm on my shoulder, and repeated a piece of a poem with great emphasis. One one of the excursions we were overtaken, and taken up into an open carriage by her ladyship and some of her companions, which afforded us a much more easy and agreeable conveyance.

I will not tell you all the remarks which I made upon this celebrated lady, else people would refrain in future from introducing me to their wives or daughters in any case; thinking I was just to come to take observations. There was one thing I heard her assert, and in the presence of her husband too; that *she was a great admirer of you.* But you need not read this to Mrs. Scott.

But of all the predicaments I ever got into, that of the theatre excelled! I suspect it was you that put it into their heads, else they would never have set as many people to work a whole forenoon, lighting up, cleaning, and arranging the scenery of the theatre that I might judge of the fitness and propriety of each. Every new scene that was displayed, my judgment was asked in full council, of every particular part. Forgive me if I knew what to say! I had often no other answer ready than scratching the crown of my head. I cursed in my heart the hour that I first put my observations on the stage on paper; and like the Yorkshire man, wished all their canvas in *h ___ bournin!*

The whole of this theatre, with all its appurtenances, is the contrivance, and executed under direction of the Hon. Colonel Campbell. He is very proud of it, as indeed he very well may, for though small, it is a most finished little piece. No man would

◁ Inveraray Castle

believe that he had such a taste for the fine arts as it is evident he hath, particularly in music and painting. I must again here draw my score, after subscribing myself, your humble servant,

James Hogg

Dear Sir, — In my last I began giving you an account of a ride which I had in company with Mr.——. but fell through the subject, and never more minded it. I will now, however, resume it, that you may see how unlucky I was in all my manoeuvres among the nobility. I told you I was mounted on a fine mare; I know not who she belonged to, but I never think it was the same that the Colonel ordered for me. She was so full of spirits that every little rivulet, and every hillock that we came at, she must necessarily make a spring over it as if she had been passing over a six bar gate. Yea, so intent was she on showing her prowess, that she bore me over dykes and ditches, than crossing which nothing could be more foreign to my inclinations or purpose. I was almost driven to desperation by her behaviour, for on coming to the outside of a high faced wall on the east side of Glen Dow, and drawing near to look at a herd of roes that were feeding within, I had taken no notice of my beast, for in a moment she sprung forward, plunged over the dyke, and landed me on the inside, among the deer. It was with much difficulty that I retained my seat, and being very angry, I whipped her against the dyke on the inside. 'Now, jump that if you can.' I was very glad to find that Mr. —— was in haste to get home. He could have no greater desire for it than I had. Although I never said much he saw my condition well enough; and always added fuel to the fire by putting the spurs to his beast on pretence of trying a trot. But then! would mine? Not a step; but galloping, rearing, and running here-away-there-away. I however got back and got rid of her with whole bones, but well bathed in sweat.

I told you that they were rather inferior sheep that I saw. I was, however, assured that the Duke had some most excellent parcels of Scottish wedders on the outer hills. These I was to have seen the ensuing day, but I thought I had seen enough about Inverary; at least before I saw as much about every place which I intended to visit, the year would be done. There was also a flock of sheep, composed of the largest Southern breeds, feeding on the castle bank. They were the strongest and best that ever I saw in Scotland, yet I was not displeased to hear that these were killed only for the use of the servants, and that the Scotch wedders were preferred for the Duke's table.

I could tell you a great deal more about this place, but I am sure you think I have descended too much to particulars already. I could tell you how struck I was on entering the library. How I could not perceive one book at all; how I always lost myself in the castle, and could never recognize the very rooms that I had lately left. And after all, there is nothing else left for me to write about. To attempt a general description after those of a Kaimes, a Pennant, and a thousand others, would be the highest presumption, and indeed I hate to write about that which everybody writes about. I shall observe (and I am afraid that you will attribute it to a spirit of contradiction, or a pride in retaining my character of singularity), that I do not much admire the *natural scenery* of Inveraray. There is a sort of sameness in the extensive view of the opposite side of the lake, and even in the lake itself, being much of a width, and destitute of islands. The hill of Duniqueich, rising above the plain, hath something of a romantic appearance, and is an exception to this general surmise; yet, strip the whole of its woods and lawns, and the scene is just common enough. But on the other hand, the artificial part is truly admirable, I had almost said inimitable. The elegant little town, the magnificent castle, the accurate taste, and discernment exhibited in the formation of the lawns and groves, many of which are striking copies of nature, and above all the great extent of the policies, ever will be admired, and never will be enough admired.

I was best pleased with the view of the castle from the lake, when it appeared embosomed in woods, and was so well contrasted with the village on one side, and a distant view of the majestic mountains in a circular range beyond it. But the greatest beauty of all is this; and it is alike applicable to the policies, to the castle, and to its inhabitants, that the nearer you approach, the better the effect. The closer the inspection, the more exalted your admiration; and the better acquaintance, the greater your esteem. And though the Duke's great age hath certainly considerably impaired the faculties of his mind, as well as his body, yet during the short time that I was in his presence, I could discover in the most trivial acts his abounded generosity and condescension. I shall only mention one or two of those.

One day at dinner Colonel Campbell said, 'My lord, why will you not try the herrings? It was for you that I ordered them.' 'Was it indeed, Jack?' said he, 'then I certainly will try them.' Which he did, and recommended then greatly. After dinner the ladies were diverting themselves by throwing crumbs of cake at the gentlemen, and at one another, to make them start when they were not observing. His Grace was growing drowsy, and one, wishing to rouse him up, called aloud in a weeping tone, 'Master, speak to Charlotte, she won't sit in peace.' The good old peer, to carry on the school jest, or rather the idea of the farmer's table, turning to that side with an important nod, said,

'Be quiet, Charlotte, I tell you,' and smiling, laid himself back on his easy chair again. These are very trifling incidents, my dear Sir, but such little family anecdotes, genuine and unaffected, the natural disposition is easier to be recognized than by a public action in the face of the world.

But if I go backward and forward this way I shall never get from Inveraray; therefore suppose me all at once on the road early in the morning on which I proceeded up Glen Aray, viewed two considerable cataracts romantically shrouded in woods, and at length arrived on the borders of Loch Awe, or Loch Howe. My plan was to take breakfast at Port Sonachan, and proceed to Oban that night, having letters to some gentleman of that country, and having a pocket travelling map, I never asked the road of anybody, at which indeed I have a particular aversion, as I am almost certain of being obliged to answer several impertinent questions as an equivalent for the favour conferred.

The road that turns to the left toward Port Sonachan is certainly in danger of being missed by a stranger, for although I was continually on the look-out for a public road to that hand, I never observed it in the least, till at last, seeing no ferry across the lake, nor road from the other side, I began to suspect that I had erred, and condescended to ask of a man if this was the road to Port Sonachan. He told me that I was above a mile past the place where the roads parted. 'And where does this lead?' said I. 'To Tyndrum, or the braes of Glenorchy,' said he; and attacked me with other questions in return, which I was in no humour to answer, being somewhat nettled at missing my intended route, and more at missing my breakfast, but knowing that whatever road I took, all was new to me, I, without standing a moment to consider of returning, held on as if nothing had happened.

About eleven a.m. I came to Dalmally in Glenorchy, where I took a hearty breakfast, but the inn has a poor appearance compared with what I have left. Some of the windows are built up with turf, and, on pretence of scarcity of fuel, they refused to kindle a fire in my apartment, although I was very wet, and pleaded movingly for one. There is nothing in this tract that I have passed deserving of particular attention. The land on the south-east side of the lake is low-lying, interspersed with gentle rising hills, and strong grassy hollows, where good crops of oats and beans were growing. On the other side the hills are high and steep and well stocked with sheep. One gentleman is introducing a stock of the Cheviot breed on a farm there this season. The had formerly been tried on a farm in the neighbourhood of the church, but the scheme was abandoned in its infancy. I am, yours, etc.

James Hogg

Dear Sir, — Leaving Dalmally, and shortly after, the high road to Tyndrum, I followed a country road which kept near the bank of the river, and led me up through the whole of that district called *the braes of Glenorchy*. At the bridge of Orchy, (or as it is spelled by some Urguhay), I rejoined the great military road leading to Fort William, and three miles farther on reached Inverournan, the mid-way stage between Tyndrum and the King's house beyond the Black Mount, where I took up my lodgings for the night.

The braes of Glenorchy have no very promising appearance, being much over-run with heath, and the north-west side rocky. But it is probable that I saw the worst part of them, their excellency as a sheep range having for a long time been established; for who, even in the south of Scotland, hath not heard of the farms of Soch and Auch!

The Orchy is a large river and there are some striking cascades in it. The glen spreads out to a fine valley on the lower parts, which are fertile, the soil on the river banks being deep, yet neither heavy nor cold. As you ascend the river the banks grow more and more narrow, till at last they terminate in heather and rocks. Beside one of the cascades which I sat down to contemplate, I fell into a long and profound sleep. The Earl of Breadalbane is the principal proprietor. I was now, at Inverournan, and got into a very Highland and rather a dreary scene. It is situated at the head of Loch Tullich, on the banks of which there yet remains a number of natural firs, a poor remembrance of the extensive woods with which its environs have once been over-run.

Amongst the fellow lodgers, I was very glad at meeting here with a Mr. McCallum, who had taken an extensive farm on the estate of Strathconnon, which I viewed last year; who informed me, that all that extensive estate was let to sheep farmers, saving a small division on the lower end, which the General had reserved for the accommodation of such of the natives as could not dispose of themselves to better advantage.

Next morning I traversed the Black Mount in company with a sailor, who entertained me with many wonderful adventures; of his being pressed, and afterwards suffering a tedious captivity in France. This indeed a most dreary region, with not one cheering prospect whereto to turn the eye. But on the right hand lies a prodigious extent of flat, barren muirs, interspersed with marshes and stagnant pools; and on the left, black rugged mountains tower to a great height, all interlined with huge wreaths of snow. The scenery is nothing improved on approaching to the King's house. There is not a green spot to be seen, and the hill behind it to the westward is still more terrific than

any to the south of it, and is little inferior to any in the famous Glencoe behind it. It is one huge cone of mishapen and ragged rocks, entirely peeled bare of all soil whatever, and all scarred with horrible furrows, torn out by the winter torrents. It is indeed a singular enough spot to have been pitched upon for a military stage and inn, where they cannot so much as find forage for a cow, but have their scanty supply of milk from a few goats, which brouse on the wide waste. There were, however, some very good black-faced wedder hoggs feeding in the middle of the Black Mount, but their colour and condition both, bespoke them to have been wintered on a richer and lower pasture, and only to have been lately turned out to that range.

After leaving the King's house I kept the high way leading to Balachulish for about two miles, and then struck off, following the old military road over the devil's stairs, which winds up the hill on one side and down on the other, and at length entered Lochaber by an old stone bridge over a water at the head of Loch Leven; and without meeting with anything remarkable, arrived at Fort William about seven o'clock p.m.

It is upwards of twenty miles from the King's house to Fort William, across the hills, and the road being extremely rough, my feet were very much bruised. The tract is wild and mountainous, the hills on the Lochaber side are amazingly high and steep, and, from the middle upward, are totally covered with small white stones. They form a part of that savage range called *the rough bounds.* Before reaching the town I passed some excellent pasture hills which were thick covered with ewes and lambs.

On arriving at Fort William I went to the house of Mr. Thomas Gillespie, who left our south country about twenty years ago, and in partnership with another, took a farm from Glengarry. His conditions were reasonable, and he being the first who introduced the improved breed of Scottish sheep into that district, his advantages were numerous, especially as his landlord, who had certainly been endowed with a liberality of mind and views extending far beyond the present moment, exacted no rent until it was raised from the farm. His companion soon gave up his share, but Mr. Gillespie, with a perseverance almost peculiar to himself, continued to surmount every difficulty, and at the expiration of every lease commonly added something to the extent of his possessions. He is now the greatest farmer in all that country, and possesseth a track of land extending from the banks of Loch Garey to the shores of the Western Ocean, upward of twenty miles.

Having lost a farm on which his principal residence stood he is now residing in Fort William, which any man would consider as very inconvenient; as so indeed it would be to any man save

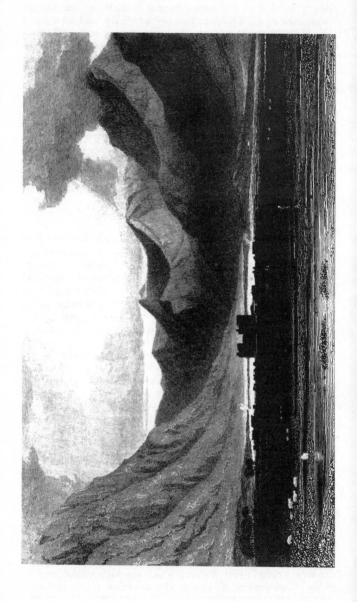

Gillespie, who is privileged with a person as indefatigable and unconquerable as his mind. He can sleep in the shepherds' cots for months together, and partake of their humble fare with as much satisfaction as the best lodgings and cheer in the world could bestow, and indeed he appears to be much happiest among his shepherds. I staid there with him and saw everything about the fortress and village that were worth looking at; and as I cannot describe the garrison, by not knowing the terms used in fortification, there is nothing that falls to be particularly noticed here, if we except the large and very ancient castle of Inverlochy. It is a large square building, with four proportionally large turrets, one at each corner, but that looking toward the north-west is much the largest; but Mr. Stuart, the tenant at Inverlochy, with whom I dined yesterday and breakfasted today, has four most elegant daughters, whom I confess I admired much more than the four turrets of the castle. The name of this place is said only twice to occur in all records of Scotland, and these at a very early period. It was there where the long respected treaty was signed between the Emperor Charlemagne and Achaius, King of Scotland. No traces of the town remain, though it is believed to have once been the capital of the Scots; nor was even the place where it stood known, until lately that on digging for stones a considerable pavement was raised behind some knolls, a little to the southward of the castle.

I was uncommonly intent on being at the top of Ben Nevis, which is agreed by all to be the highest mountain in the British Islands, but the mist never left its top for two hours during my stay. I had once set out and proceeded a good way toward it when the clouds again settled on its summit and obliged me to return.

Fort-William, or Maryburgh as it was formerly called, is situated on the side of Loch Yel, immediately at the confluence of the Nevis; and as the loch will admit ships of any burden, we might expect that from its favourable situation, it would be the mart of the whole Western Highlands; whereas it is destitute of trade and manufactures, nor was there a vessel in the harbour; and there is thrice as much traffic and barter carried on at some of the fishing villages.

I must now depart, but remain, Sir, your faithful

Ettrick Shepherd

Lochaber
Monday, 6th June

Dear Sir, — Having breakfasted early we, viz., Mr. Gillespie,

◁ Inverlochy Castle

Mr. William Stuart of Inverlochy, and *Master James Hogg,* left Fort William. Leaving the military road, we crossed the Lochy above the old castle. It is a large, dark river, and there is a good salmon fishing in it, which is farmed by Mr. Stuart at a high rent, from the Duke of Gordon; but, like most of the northern rivers in the Western Highlands, hath failed unaccountably for two years past. We kept by the side of the river and Loch Lochy until we came to the river Arkaig; then following its course, we reached Achnacarry, where we spent the middle of the day, viewing the new castle of Lochiel, the building of which was then going briskly on, conducted by Mr. John Gillespie, architect; a respectable young man, possessed of much professional knowledge, who kept us company during our stay.

The castle is on an extensive scale and promiseth to be a stately structure. It is founded within a few yards of the site of the ancient one, the residence of the brave Lochiel who was wounded at the battle of Culloden, and escaped with Prince Charles to France. This pile was reduced to ashes by the Duke of Cumberland's forces in seventeen hundred and forty-six, and the marks of the fire are still too visible, not only on the remaining walls of the house and offices, but also on a number of huge venerable trees, which the malevolent brutes had kindled. Some of these, although the heart was burnt out of them, still continued to flourish.

It is indeed a very remarkable spot to have chosen for erecting such a princely residence upon, being entirely obscured amongst woods and wild mountains, which deprive it of any prospect whatever. There is no public road near it, nor is it accessible by a carriage at present, yet I could not but in my heart greatly applaud Lochiel for the choice, not only as it was the seat of his noble ancestors, and adorned by a garden inferior to few in the Highlands, if again in repair, as well as by sundry elegant avenues, formed and shaded by trees of great age and beauty; but also on account of the utility of having his family residence in the midst of his extensive estate, in the very place where roads and bridges are most wanted, and where he can encourage by his example, elegance and improvements among the better part of his tenants, (many of whom are substantial, intelligent men of his own name,) give employment to the meaner sort, and assistance to the indigent. The whole scene is romantic beyond conception. On the banks of Loch Arkaig to beyond it there are large forests of wood, which in many places are perfect thickets. In these woods the Pretender skulked for some time, attended by a very few followers indeed, and was often in great danger of being surprised. He was in an island in Loch Arkaig when the corpse was found which was mistaken for the body of his dear Lochiel, and pained him beyond measure. It turned out to be only that of a friend of his. Lochiel remained safe and almost unmolested, amongst the wilds which separate

Athol and Badenoch.

About one o'clock we took our leave of Mr. Stuart, Mr. Gillespie, the architect, and a Captain Cameron who had joined us, proceeded by the way of Glenkekuich, a most shocking road, where I thought Mr. Gillespie should have lost his horse. We were shown the very spot in this track where Prince Charles met a band of dragoons in search of him, and was forced to squat among the heath until they passed by, and was so near them that he heard their talk.

While traversing the scenes where the patient sufferings of the one party, and the cruelties of the other, were so affectingly displayed, I could not help being a bit of a Jacobite in my heart, and blessing myself that, in those days, I did not exist, or I should certainly have been hanged.

This country of Lochaber, which I now left behind me, excels all in those regions for lofty mountains and fertile valleys. It is upon the whole a very interesting and diversified scene, and were it not for my oath of brevity, I should certainly launch out into a particular description of it. The famous mountain of Ben Nevis, the king of the Grampians, rises 4380 feet above the level of the sea, and hugs in its uncouth bosom, huge masses of everlasting snow, and all that range, both to the east and west, is wild and savage beyond measure. The valleys are interspersed with numbers of cottages, as also a good gentlemen's seats, and substantial houses belonging to the principal tenants, or rather tacksmen, as they are there denominated. It is watered by the Nevis, the Lochy, the Spare, and the Arkaig; and by numberless smaller streams. In the more remote glens there are large and beautiful woods. The estate of Letterfinlay, and some of Lochiel's glens are beautiful for sheep pasturage, but the bulk of the hills are rough and ugly. There are a great many of the sheep not yet of a proper breed, and consequently not excellent, yet numbers of very strong wedders are annually driven to the south from some of these parts.

It is certainly a place where a great deal may be done, and where a great deal will be done. The tillage is capable of being greatly extended, and if proper encouragement be given in the new leases, (for the most part of Lochaber is out of lease,) it will be extended, as well as improved. As it is all on a Western exposure, and intersected by extensive arms of the sea, so remarkable for the humidity and freshness of its breezes, it suffers very little from storms of lying snow, for although the mountains are so very high, the bottoms of the glens seldom rise to any great height above the level of the sea; so that in this important matter of snow storms the sheep farmer is safe.

The greater part of this district is certainly calculated only for the rearing of these useful animals, sheep, yet there are still many places not stocked with them, or but very partially so. But as there is now such a number of enlightened farmers in the

country and its neighbourhood, experience, the most effectual teacher, will soon convince the natives of their real interest.

The Duke of Gordon, and Lochiel, are the principal proprietors. Glen Nevis, and Letterfinlay are also considerable estates. His Grace's lands are rather overstocked with poor people.

It appears as if all these highland hills not many years ago, had been valued only in proportion to the game produced, as the wildest and most uninhabitable countries never fail to belong to the greatest men. The Duke of Gordon in particular, possesseth an immense range of these savage districts, extending in a confused chain from the Eastern to the Western Oceans. Take a journey through Lochaber, Laggan, Badenoch, Glenmore, and Strathaven, and when you come to a wild, desert glen, (and you will not miss *enow* of them,) you need not trouble yourself to enquire who is the proprietor. You may take it forgranted it is the 'Duke of Gordon,' and you would scarcely refrain from the Englishman's apostrophe to Invercauld, 'D—n that fellow, I believe he hath got the whole highlands.'

I promised to you at the first when I began to write to you on this subject that I would give my sentiments freely of men and things, whether they were right or wrong. And I have to confess to you that my expectations with respect to the opening of the proposed canal, differ widely from those of almost every other person. I have too high an opinion of the energy of the British Legislature to have any doubts of its accomplishment, but I will venture to predict that although you should live an hundred years after its completion, you will never see it a well-frequented canal; nay, that you shall never see the tonnage pay the interest of the sum thereon expended. You will be apt to tear this letter or fling it away in a rage, but I charge you do not, but keep it, and when you die tell Walter to keep it until the result shall prove the absurdity of my ideas, and then do anything with it you please. I will in my next acquaint you with my simple reasons for this belief, as well as my hopes of its utility, which nevertheless in one sense are very sanguine.

In the meantime, believe me, Sir, your faithful,

Ettrick Shepherd

*Inchlaggan
Monday 6th June*

My Dear Sir,—I know that you will reject my arguments on the Caledonian Canal as futile and inadmissible, but I do not care. Enough hath been said and written on the other side, therefore I shall state my reason and let the event do justice to the merits of each calculator.

And in the first place I think that the greatest number of vessels may be supposed to pass by it from East to West, because those bound from America to any of the ports on the continent of Europe, or Eastern coast of Britain, could, while in the open Atlantic, steer with as much ease and safety by Orkney, as through amongst the Hebrides into Lochiel. Now, to counteract this I must inform you of a circumstance which you probably have never thought of, but to the truth of which every sailor coastwise, and every attentive shepherd in Scotland can bear witness, that in a term of three years the wind always blows at least two-thirds of the time from that quarter of the compass lying betwixt South and West. If these two points are allowed, as in part they must, how is it possible to navigate these narrow lochs with a continual head wind, where no tides are, to carry them on piecemeal, as in the sounds of the ocean? But granting, what is not possible, that the winds as well as the navigation should be equal from each side of the island, yet, in Loch Ness especially, the hills spreading at each end, and the whole length of the lake being confined between two steep ridges of mountains, the wind must necessarily blow either straight up or straight down the lake, consequently the sailor must enter the narrow gut with the disagreeable assurance of having all the winds from one half of the globe right ahead of him. I acknowledge myself to be quite ignorant of the principles of navigation, but the idea of conducting a heavy ship in this case betwixt two rocky shores never above a mile, and often not above half a mile separated, appears to me a desperate undertaking.

The argument that there are a number of safe anchorings, is of small avail either for safety or despatch. They are indeed a safeguard against a continued storm, but none against sudden squalls, which amongst the mountains and gaps are as terrible as they are unceasing; and it would be no very agreeable circumstance for a heavy ship to be overtaken by one of these, augmented with the united gusts from several glens while endeavouring to tack, so hard upon a lea shore as they must of necessity be, if indeed they get any stretch at all.

I wish from my heart, sir, that these impediments may be only imaginary, and I shall try to console myself with the assurance that they were all weighed by more experienced heads ere ever the experiment was seriously thought of.

In one case I am sure it will in time prove a national benefit, namely by drawing a numerous population into that important isthmus, formed by nature to be the seat of trade betwixt the countries to the south and north of it. At different places along it, and at different seasons, there should be large trysts established for cattle and sheep, corresponding with those in the south, that the farmers in the highlands and islands to the north of that may not be so entirely in the power of interested drovers, who, though an useful set of men, get a great deal of the cattle and sheep in those distant countries on their own terms. They are so far removed from any principal market that the people for the most part, rather than set out toward the banks of the Forth with their own small quantity, prefer such offers as come to their own doors, though often very inferior, there being also a risk of late and uncertain payment, whereas were they sure of even a moderate price for driving them to the banks of Glenmore-na-h-alabin, it would be a great encouragement. Besides, they would from the same place need frequent supplies of many of the necessaries, and all the luxuries of life, as from thence they could have easy conveyances by land or water.

But you will readily ask, from whence shall this population and increased traffic proceed, if, as you say, it is not to be influenced by an extensive business carried on by the canal? My dear sir, you are not aware what prodigious numbers of poor people drag on a wretched existence in those distant glens and islands, who are scarcely privileged, as we would think, with one of the comforts or conveniences of life. As for instance, what do you think of upwards of ten thousand people subsisting on the dreary and distant Isle of Lewis, which with the exception of a very inconsiderable part, is one extensive morass; while the whole rent of the island, although lately advanced, does not reach to a thousand pounds. This is but one instance out of many, and it may well be supposed, nay, I am *certain,* that there are many thousands in these countries whose condition cannot be *worsed* unless they are starved to death. Now, only conceive what numbers of these, from first to last, will be employed here before the great canal and the roads be finished, where they will mix with more enlightened people, form acquaintances, contract marriages, and thus enlarge their connections in the place. New lights and advantages, both real and imaginary, will daily present themselves to their imaginations, as acquirable in that place where conditions have been ameliorated by their application to labour, so that we may presume that a small encouragement held out to such as choose to settle in the great glen, will readily be accepted of by numbers.

Perhaps a prejudiced fellow like me, unconscious of the utility of such a naval communication, may think that one third of the money laid out upon the great canal, would have been better employed in purchasing land to be let out in feus to those tribes and families annually, vomited out by their own native, inhospitable shores, and forced to seek for a more certain means of subsistence in the Western world, in search of which, many a brave Scot has sunk broken-hearted and forlorn, to his long home, and has found the wished-for resting place only in the New World, beyond death and the grave, while the last idea

that floated on his distempered mind, and the last words that wavered on his tongue, were those of regard for his native land.

And after all, if something is not done to provide asylums for these brave men and their families, and to establish woollen manufactures, they may live to see their *roads grow green, and a blue scum settle on their canal;* and to hear themselves addressed in the language of Scripture, Matthew, xxiii., and 23. 'Woe be to you, ye blind guides, who strain at a gnat, and swallow a camel! These things ought ye to have done, and not to have left the other undone.''

Rest assured of this, my dear sir; that men, sheep, and fish, are the great staple commodities of Scotland; and that, though a number of other improvements *may* contribute to its emolument, yet whatever tends more particularly to encourage or improve any of these *will* do it.

I shall probably have occasion to treat more of this in another place, and shall again proceed on my journey.

On reaching Glengarry the first place we came to was Greenfield, possessed by Mr. McDonald. The house was really a curiosity. It was built of earth, and the walls were all covered with a fine verdure, but on calling we were conducted into a cleanly and neat-looking room, having a chimney, and the walls being plastered. The ladies, Mrs. McDonald and her sister, were handsome and genteelly dressed, although unapprised of our arrival, unless by the second sight. They were very easy and agreeable in their manners, and very unlike the *outside* of their habitation. The family were Roman Catholics, and kept a young priest among them, but he had lately been obliged to abscond for some misdemeanour in marrying a couple secretly. He was much lamented by the whole family, but by none so much as Miss Flora.

We saw Mr. McDonald's ewes gathered. He hath an excellent stock of sheep. We got a late dinner, drank plenty of punch, etc., and at night crossed the Garry to Inchlaggan, a farm of Mr. Gillespie's and took up our lodging with his shepherd.

I remain, your most affectionat servt.,

James Hogg

Loch Duich
Friday, 10th June

Dear Sir,—I took leave of you in my last at Inchlaggan in Glen Garry, where Gillespie and I slept together in a small stooped bed, having neither sides nor cover. We spent the whole of next day among his sheep, came back to the same lodgings at night,

◁ Loch Oich and Invergarry

and the third day I took my leave of him, very well pleased with what I had seen. It is believed by most people that I am too partial to the Highlands, and that they will not produce such stocks as I affirm that they will. Let them only take an impartial view of Glengarry and accuse me if they can. The superiority of its grazings to those of a great many other Highland countries, is in no wise discernable to the beholder, yet the stocks of sheep upon it are equal in quality to those of any country in the south of Scotland. Gillespie hath one farm completely stocked with the finest Cheviot breed, which thrive remarkably well. These he bought on the Border, at the exhorbitant prices of sixteen shillings for each lamb, and twenty-four for each of the hoggs, or year-olds. The lambs came all safe home, but three of the hoggs fell by the way. They went home on the seventeenth day from their leaving Rule Water, a distance upwards of two hundred miles by the drove road. He intends breeding wedders from them for his farms of Glenqueich, but to sell ewe lambs until he sees how the wedders thrive. All the stocks of sheep on Glengarry are good, the farms belong all to Mr. Gillespie, or have been possessed by him, consequently the sheep are all of his breed. The ground lets very high. Alexander MacDonald, Esquire, of Glengarry, is the proprietor. A great part of the land is very coarse. but the heather, grass, and all sorts of herbage grow luxuriantly, and spring up to a great length. There is a considerable part of flat ground, and some woods on the lower parts, and the hills are lower and of easier ascent than those of Lochaber.

Leaving Inchlaggan and Mr. Gillespie, I travelled through an exceedingly rough country. The day was wet and misty, and there was no track of a road, or if there was I did not happen on it. I crossed Glen-Loyn hard by the mouth of the loch; went through a farm belonging to Ratachan, which was very coarse land, being overrun with moss, but on which there was a very excellent stock of wedders feeding. After a most fatiguing march, I came in upon Loch-Cluny, and crossing the water at its head, I joined the old military road at the very green spot where Dr. Johnson rested, and first conceived the design of transmitting his tour to posterity.

I came to the house of Cluny, which is a solitary steading in that wild glen. It is a change-house, but I did not know, nor even thought of it, although I had much need of some refreshment. There were sundry workmen employed in mounting a house, at whom I only enquired the road; but I had not proceeded many miles until I grew faintish with hunger, having got nothing that day, saving a little pottage at the shepherd's house early in the morning.

The road down to Glen Shiel is entirely out of repair and remarkably rough and stony, and I was quite exhausted before I reached any other house, which was not until about the setting of the sun. I at length came to a place where there had been a great number of houses, which were now mostly in ruins, the estate being all converted into sheep-walks. I went into the best that remained, and immediately desired them to give me some meat. I was accosted by an old man who declared that they had nothing that they could give me. I told him that it was with much difficulty I had got that length, and that I was not able to proceed further unless I got something to eat, and desired him to order me something, for which I was willing to pay whatever he should demand. He persisted in his denial of having anything that he could give me, telling me that I was not two miles from the change-house. I was obliged to go away, although I suspected that I would not *make* the inn, but before I had gone far a young man came out and called me back. He was in a poor state of health, and had risen out of his bed on hearing the dialogue between the old man and me. He conducted me into a kind of room, and presented me with plenty of bread, whey, butter, and cheese. In the state that I was in, I durst only take a very little, for which he refused to take anything, declaring that I was very welcome, and that he wished the fare had been better, for my sake. I was greatly refreshed, and proceeded on my way. Before it was quite dark I reached the inn of Inver shiel, or Shiel-house, held by a Mr. Johnston from Annandale.

It is a large, slated house, but quite out of repair, and the accommodations are intolerably bad. The lower apartments are in utter confusion, and the family resides in the diningroom above. Consequently, they have only one room into which they thrust promiscuously every one that comes. The plaister of this being all discoloured, and full of chinks, the eye is continually tracing the outlines of monstrous animals and hobgoblins upon it. I got the best bed, but it was extremely hard, and the clothes had not the smell of roses. It was also inhabited by a number of little insects common enough in such places, and no sooner had I made a lodgement in their hereditary domains than I was attacked by a thousand strong. But what disturbed me much worse than all, I was awaked during the night by a whole band of Highlanders, both male and female, who entered my room, and fell to drinking whisky with great freedom. They had much the appearance of a parcel of vagabonds, which they certainly were, but as the whole discourse was in Gaelic I knew nothing of what it was concerning, but it arose by degrees as the whisky operated, to an insufferable noise. I had by good fortune used more precaution that night than usual, having put my watch and all my money into my waistcoat and hid it beneath my head. I also took my thorn-staff into the bed with me, thereby manifesting a suspicion that I had never shewed before. I bore all this uproar with patience for nearly two hours in the middle of the night, until, either by accident or design, the candle was extinguished, when every one getting up a great stir comm-

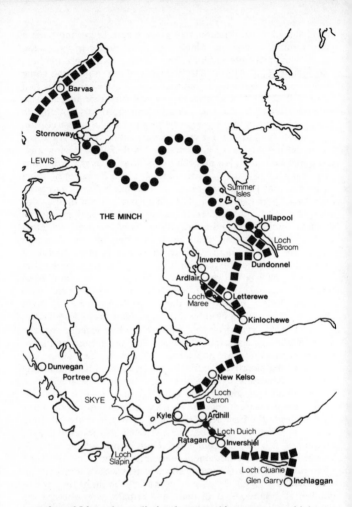

enced, and I heard one distinctly ransacking my coat which was
hanging upon a chair at a little distance from the bed. I cared
not much for that, thinking that he could get nothing there, but
not knowing where this might end I sprung to my feet in the
bed, laid hold of my thorn-staff, and bellowed aloud for light. It
was a good while ere this could be procured, and when it came
the company were all gone but three men, who were making
ready to lie down in another bed in the same room. I repri-
manded the landlord with great bitterness for suffering such a
disturbance in the room where I slept, and received for answer
that all would be quiet now. They were all gone before I got up
next morning, and it was not until next night that I perceived

I had lost a packet of six letters which I carried, to as many gentlemen in Sutherland, and which prevented me effectually from making the tour of that large and little-frequented county. These being rolled up in a piece of paper by themselves and lodged in my breast pocket, some one of the gang had certainly carried off in expectation that it was something of more value. Next day I went to the house of Ratagan or Ratachan, possessed by Donald Macleod, Esquire, to whom I had a letter of introduction. He received me with that open, unaffected, cordiality which is a leading trait in his character, and without that state and ceremony which is certainly often carried too far by the Highland people, and which I hate above all things. His conversation was much confined to that which suited me best, namely, the sheep-farming. He hath extensive concerns in this way, being possessed of two large farms here in Glen Shiel, exclusive of that of Armidel in Glen Elg, or as they pronounce it, Glen Ellig, which he had lately taken at the yearly rent of £600. He had the best wedder hoggs without exception that I saw in my whole journey. He bought them as lambs from Killetur in Glenfalloch. He remembered Dr. Johnson and Mr. Boswell, and told me sundry anecdotes relating to them. His mother is still alive, a woman of a great age yet quite healthy. She dined and supped with us, but did not converse any, which was probably owing to her inaccuracy in the English language. She is the same of whom Dr. Johnson makes honourable mention in his tour. We had plenty of music and some dancing, his eldest daughter being a most charming performer on the pianoforte, and Mr. Gordon, the family teacher, equally expert at playing on the violin.

I would willingly have staid some days in this agreeable family, but was afraid that Macleod's attention to me would retard the shearing of his flocks, for which he had everthing in readiness; so hearing that the Rev. John Macrae was bound for Ardhill in Lochalsh, I took my leave in order to accompany him. Ratachan accompanied me to the manse, and left me in charge with the parson. Here the company at dinner consisted of twelve, which, saving the old minister and I, were all ladies; mostly young ones, and handsome. As soon as dinner was over, we entered into a boat, viz, Miss Flora Macrae of Ardintoul, and her aunt, the parson, and me. Miss Flora was tall, young and handsome, and being dressed in a dark riding habit, with a black helmet and red feather, made a most noble figure. I was very happy on hearing that she was to be passenger. We had six rowers in the boat, and we sat in a row astern, the two ladies being *middlemost*. There being a sharp breeze straight in our face, as soon as we were seated, Mr. Macrae spread his great coat on the old lady and himself. This was exactly as I wished it, and I immediately wrapped Miss Flora in my shepherd's plaid, and though I was always averse to sailing, I could willingly have proceeded in this position for at least a week. We were at length obliged to put ashore here, about the middle of Loch Duich, at the place to which the boat belongs, but as I have drawn out this letter to an enormous length, I will bid you adieu for the present — Yours, etc.,

James Hogg

Dear Sir, — No sooner had the boat touched the shore than we were met by the owner, who was in uncommonly high spirits, this being his wedding-day. He insisted on our staying to drink tea with him, and to induce us to comply told us that if we staid we should have the boat and crew all the way, but if we refused to countanance him we should walk all the the rest of the way on foot. There was no resisting this proposal so we went ashore, drank tea with the young couple and their friends, and so strongly did they press us to drink whisky, that had I been in company with any other than the minister and Miss Flora, they had certainly persuaded me to fill myself drunk. We then marched into the barn, where the music was playing, and joined with avidity in their Highland reels until remined by Mr. Macrae of approaching night, when we all again resumed our former berths in the boat and proceeded with as much cheerfulness as can be conceived. Mr. Macrae hath the character of being a very able divine, for which I cannot avouch, but he certainly is a most jocose and entertaining companion.

The family of Ardintoul being all Roman Catholics, thinking to lead me into a scrape when in the boat —

'Have you any priests in your country, Mr. Hogg?' said he.

'We have some very superior parish ministers in my country, sir,' said I.

'It is Popish priests that I mean,' said he, 'I hope you are not plagued with any of that wicked set.'

'There are none of that persuasion in my neighbourhood,' said I, 'saving the Earl of Traquair and his family, who keep a priest among them.'

'Ah! You are well quit of them,' said he, 'we are terribly plagued with them hereabouts! They are a bad set of people! Do you not think, Mr. Hogg, that they are very bad people?'

I began to suspect him. 'I don't know, sir,' said I, 'there are certainly worthy persons of every persuasion. I approve greatly of a person keeping to the religion in which he is brought up, and I would never esteem a man the less because he thought differently from me.'

The old lady then began to attack him, asking if ever he had found them to be ill neighbours.

'Oh! It won't do, it won't do!' said he, 'I thought of leading Mr. Hogg into a little abuse of you, as I once did a tide-waiter at your brother's house, who ignorant that his kind entertainer and the family were all of that persuasion, fell on and abused the Papists without either mercy or discretion, putting Ardintoul's great patience severly to the test. He was suffered, however, to depart in his error.'

We at length set the ladies ashore and took our leave of them. I gave Miss Flora two letters to her father, and promised to dine with them the next day. Mr. Macrae, after taking leave of them, cried out shrewdly, 'Now farewell, Miss Flora! Without pretending to the spirit of prophecy I could tell you who you will dream of to-night.'

Considering of what inflammable materials my frame is composed, it was probably very fortunate that I was disappointed of ever seeing Miss Macrae again, as I might have felt the inconvenience of falling in love with an object in that remote country. I received word today at Ardhill that she was taken very ill of the influenza, then raging in Kintail with great violence, and that Ardintoul, her father, was confined to bed, so that I was persuaded by the company to relinquish my intended visit as inconvenient.

About eight o'clock, p.m., we landed at Ardhill, the house of the Rev. Alexander Downie, minister of Lochalsh, to whom I had likewise a letter of introduction, from his cousin, Colin Mackenzie, Esquire, W.S. This district of Glen Shiel which I now had left, is like the greatest part of the countries on that coast, very mountainous. Although the whole parish is thus denominated, Glen Shiel properly is that straight glen which terminates at the outer end of Loch Duich, and, stretching to the south-east, includes a great part of Glen Morison, and on the east is bounded by the heights of Affarick, one of the branches of the Glass. The mountains are very high and steep, especially those of them most contiguous to the sea. They are very rocky and often bare of soil, but the rocks are everywhere interlined with green stripes covered with sweet and nutritious grasses, which being continually moistened with fresh showers from the Atlantic, are preserved in verdure a great part of the year. The snow never continues long on these mountains except on the heights, the frosts are seldom intense, but the winds and rains àre frequent and terrible. You will be apt to suppose that all that western coast will be alike exposed to these, but there is, according to the inhabitants, who must know best, a very great difference. Wherever the mountains towards the shore rise to a great height there the rains are most frequent and descend in most copious abundance; and it is observed that places in the same lattitude with these mountains on the eastern coast are very rarely visited with any rain from the west. It is

a fact that these mountains attract the clouds as well as inter-
cept and break them, as I shall show in a future letter. But there
is no part of the Highlands to which the climate is better
adapted than Glen Shiel, the hills being so steep and bare of
soil, and so dry naturally, that without a constant rain they
would soon wither and decay.

The mountains of Glen Shiel have been under sheep for some
years, of which I shall have occasion to treat farther at another
time. The banks of Loch Duich are as yet mostly stocked with
cattle, and there is part arable land, which although not productive of weighty crops, produces them without much uncertainty.
Two gentlemen had sowed potatoe oats this season which
looked very well, and promise to answer the climate if they are
cut in time, before they are shaken by the winds. The tract of
land stretching alongst the southern shore of Loch Duich,
although in the parish of Glen Shiel, is called Letterfern. The
banks of this lake, which is an inlet of the sea from the Sound of
Skye, presents to the traveller many scenes of natural beauty.

We sailed close under the walls of the ancient castle of
Ellendonan, or the Sea-fort, the original possession of the
family of the Mackenzies, Earls of Seaforth, and from which
they draw their title. The history of their first settling in that
country after the battle of Largs, of the manner of their working
themselves into the possession of Kintail, Loch Alsh, and Glen
Shiel, and afterwards of Lewis, was all related to me by Mr.
Macrae with great precision. It is curious and entertaining, but
full of intrigue and deceit, and much too tedious for me to write,
as it would of itself furnish matter for a volume. The battle of
Glen Shiel did not happen until some years after the battles of
Sherriffmuir and Preston, and fought near the boundaries of
Seaforth's country, in a strait pass between the mountains of
Glen Shiel. The combatants were our King's troops and a body
of about five or six hundred Highlanders and Spaniards, headed
by the brave but misguided Earl of Seaforth.

The Spaniards, sensible of their destitute situation engaged
reluctantly; but seeing the intrepidity of the brave Macraes and
Mackenzies, they maintained the combat stoutly for some time.
The Highlanders say that the commander of the King's troops
was killed, and that they were upon the very point of giving way
when the Spaniards threw down their arms and surrendered,
and that then the clansmen were obliged to betake themselves
to flight, carrying with them from the field their lord, danger-
ously wounded. He was then obliged to go into exile, and his
lands were forfeited to the Crown, but the bold and tenacious
inhabitants absolutely refused paying rents to any man excepting their absent chief, and all the endeavours of Government to
collect them were baffled with disgrace. Their agents were
repelled and some of them slain, while the rents were regularly
transmitted to the earl, and it showed the great lenity of our

Government that they were not made examples of, and that the annals of that age were not stained with the massacre of Glen Shiel, in addition to that of Glencoe.

I remain, Sir, Yours for ever,

James Hogg

Ardhill
Saturday 11th June

Dear Sir, — As I arrived at Ardhill on the Friday preceding the celebration of the sacrament of the Supper in this place, I was introduced to a whole houseful of ministers and elders. As Mr. Downie, however, kept an excellent board, and plenty of the best foreign spirits, we had most excellent fare, and during that night and the next day, which you know was the preparation day, we put ourselves into as good a state of preparation for the evening solemnity as good cheer would make us. To introduce you a little into our company, I will give you a sketch of our ministers.

Mr. Downie, our landlord, is a complete gentleman, nowise singular for his condescension. Besides the good stipend and glebe of Loch Alsh, he hath a chaplaincy in a regiment, and extensive concerns in farming, both on the mainland and in the isles, and is a great improver in the breeds both of cattle and sheep. Mr. Macrae of Glenshiel, as I before hinted, though advanced in years, is a most shrewd and good humoured gentleman, whose wit never tends to mortify anybody, but only to raise the laugh against them. Mr. M'Queen of Applecross is a quiet, unassuming man. He is from the Isle of Skye, and is son to the minister there, who was so highly approved of by Dr. Johnson. Mr. Colin M'Iver of Glen Elig, was here, but was obliged to set off for Lewis to see a brother who was on his death-bed. He is a man whose presence commands respect. But the most extraordinary personage of the of the whole is a Mr. Roderick Macrae, preacher of the Gospel at Ferriden. He is certainly a man of considerable abilities, but his manner is the most singular, and his address the most awkward that were ever combined in the same being. He keeps his head in a continual up-and-down motion, somewhat resembling a drake approaching his mate, or a horse which has been struck violently on the head, and who is afraid that you are going to repeat the blow; and at each of these capers, he gives a strait wink with his eyes; and whoever is speaking, he continues at every breath to repeat a kind of wince, signifying that he is taking notice, or that he wisheth you to proceed. Against this man all their shafts were levelled, often armed with the most keen and ready wit.

Parish ministers in a country place, being so used to harangue others, and to see whole multitudes turn up the white of the eye to their discourse, are themselves so little used to listen to others, that though they are often the best informed men of the place and excellent single companions, very seldom is it that they can make themselves agreeable in a larger company, as they only wish to be listened unto, and never condescend to take any heed to that which is said by others. It was by such a behaviour that this young man drew on himself the ridicule of the others in one united torrent, for, as he engrossed at least one half of the whole conversation, and as the rest were all his seniors, all of them were chagrined at being superseded in their favourite amusement of divulging their sentiments.

Mr. Downie, who is certainly a very clever man, as well as a great scholar, took every opportunity to mortify and crush him. Old Macrae set the whole table in a roar of laughter at him a hundred times; and indeed, I think I never laughed so much at a time in my life. He had lately published a pamphlet, entitled 'A Dissertation on Miracles,' some copies of which were in the room, and proved matter for considerable rebuffs. The piece itself was sound, simple reasoning and common sense, but every possible method was taken to wrest the sentiments, that the ideas might be turned into ridicule. In particular, they objected, and not without considerable show of reason, that the whole of it went directly to counteract the intent of its publication, which being to confute the arguments of Mr. Hume, it would readily induce the country people, many of whom had never heard of Mr. Hume nor his book, to search for and consult it, when there was little doubt of their finding his arguments stronger and more impressive than those set down in the pamphlet.

Mr. Downie made me acquainted with the book and its author in the following brief manner. Taking it off a back table, 'Here,' said he, 'Mr. Hogg, is a dissertation on *Miracles*, composed, written, and published by our friend Mr. Rory there, a certain evidence that miracles have not ceased.' Mr. Roderick, however, stood his ground powerfully against them all, for he still kept his good temper — the best mark of an antagonist — persevered in his untoward motions, and in maintaining the excellence of his arguments.

Among such a number of literary men I could not miss getting a good deal of intelligence respecting the state of the countries in their different parishes, but I dare not state one article as received from any of them; for, judging it ill manners to make out a journal of it in their company, I committed it wholly to my memory, where setting it so effectually afloat on rum-punch, when I come to collect it I can only fish out some insignificant particles. There were no ladies in the room but Mrs. Downie, a beautiful little woman, exceedingly attentive to the accommodation of her guests, especially such as were bashful and backward. She was one of the Miss M'Kinnons of Corrialachan, in Skye.

Today being Saturday there was an extraordinary multitude assembled to hear sermon. I thought I never saw as many on the same occasion by one half, which convinced me that the lower classes of Kintail are devout. The men are generally tall and well made, and have good features. The woman of the lower class are very middling.

The two Messrs. Macrae preached; the one in Gaelic at the tent, and the other in the church in English. By far the greatest congregation attended at the tent. There was, however, a considerable number of the more genteel people in the church. I was persuaded, much against my inclination, by the importunities of the minister, to officiate as precentor in the church, otherwise he must have acted in that capacity himself.

On returning to dinner our company was considerably augmented, so much that the circle went in contact with the walls of the dining-room. This made me alter my resolution of staying on the Sacrament, for fear of proving an incumbrance, which I would always avoid. After dinner Mr. M'Kinnon, a young gentleman from Skye, and I, set off for the house of Auchtertyre, inhabited by Donald Macdonald, Esquire, of Barrisdale. I saw and spoke with him and Mrs. Macdonald at church, and expected that they would invite me which, however, they did not. The Highland gentlemen expect strangers to call without being invited. I did not know this, but went to see the man merely because I liked him, for in conformity to a maxim of old Advocate Mackintosh's, '*I never like a man if I don't like his face.*'

We met a most kind welcome from Barrisdale, whom we found in the midst of a great room-full of ladies, with only one or two young gentlemen, of whom he complained that they would not drink any. I have met again with the families of Ratachan and Glenshiel. The drinking was renewed on our entering, which before had been going to fall into disuse, and we soon became remarkably merry, screwed up the fiddles, and raised a considerable dance. It was here that I ventured to sing my song of Donald Macdonald, and although afraid to venture it I could not forbear, it is so appropriate, Barrisdale being one of the goodliest and boldest looking men anywhere to be met with. It was so highly applauded here that I think I shall sing it very often during the rest of my journey.

By this excursion we missed the prayers and exhortations at the manse, whither we returned to supper. The supper did not, however, close the excercise of the evening, but as it is certainly time for me to close this letter, I shall write farewell.

The Ettrick Shepherd

89

Dear Sir, — Leaving Ardhill early in the morning, and climbing the mountains towards the country of Loch Carron, I took a last look of Kintail, not without regret, for I really admired the inhabitants as well as the country, It is subdivided into several small districts, such as Glen Shiel, Glen Croe, Glen Elchaig, Letterfeirn and Loch Alsh, but the whole country is included in the general name of Kintail, or Lord Seaforth's country. What a great pity it is that his circumstances have made it necessary for him to mutilate so fine and so compact an estate by selling Loch Alsh, the richest, and most beautiful part of it.

The whole is an excellent pasture country, and excels all that I visited on the whole Western coast of Scotland and the Isles, for the richness of its pasture, if we except some parts of Skye. The black cattle are a very handsome breed, but unless in Glen-Shiel the sheep farming is by no means become general as yet. Barrisdale and Ardintoul have both commenced it, bringing hoggs from the south. I am very apprehensive that on being first stocked with sheep, the braxy will prove very destructive, for exclusive of the *toth,* caused by such members of cattle feeding and lying upon it, the grasses are naturally flatulent, and the herbage indigestable, and as they have not all sea-marsh to lay them upon, the only preventatives that are in their power must be the effect produced by burning the ground well, and in the proper management of their flocks.

In the first place, as to burning their ground, they must be careful to lay waste by fire all or the greatest part of their heather that is upon clay or gravelly soils; such parts being without fail, of all others the most instrumental in raising the braxy. Whether this proceeds from the nature of the heather itself, or from the long, foul grass that is always fostered about the roots of bushes, I cannot so certainly determine. Perhaps it ariseth from both causes united; but in either respect the fire is an effectual remedy, and as the ground becomes annually more thickly covered with sweet blades, and sprays of grass which owing to the ashes with which it is sprinkled and impregnated, are all rather of a purgative nature, thus by the operation of burning alone, the very spots that were before the bane of the flocks are rendered the most conducive in preserving their health. Even when the young heather again begins to sprout, it is not for many years of a hurtful nature, but is a soft, and most palatable food. And as it is only in the first year of the sheep's age that they are subject in any great degree to this destructive malady, methods may be pursued in the arrangement of the flocks which may be greatly instrumental in allaying its virulence. But as I rather wish to study brevity in these letters I shall reserve my suggestions on that head until a more suitable opportunity.

Loch Duich is an excellent fishing station, but there are neither villages, roads, bridges, nor post office, in the whole country. The gentlemen employ a runner to Loch Carron, where a foot-post arrives once a week from Inverness by the way of Strathconon, where he must often be detained by storms and flooded waters. The old military road, which runs through a corner of the upper parts of the country, leading to Fort-Augustus is, as I before observed, almost impassible, not having been repaired for ages; and all the others are entirely in a state of nature, being merely small tracks worn on the surface by the frequent pressure of the traveller's foot. In particular it was alleged to me that a road leading from the head of Loch Luang through the braes of Balloch into Strathglass would be of the greatest utility to both countries by opening the straightest and quickest communication betwixt the two seas.

Kintail is not much appropriated for the purposes of agriculture. It is indeed interspersed by vallies of small extent which are not of themselves unfertile, but the boisterousness of the weather, renders their produce very precarious.

The mountains in Glenshiel and Seaforth's forest viewed from the hills of Loch Alsh, although lofty and rugged have a verdant appearance. The mountains of Skye contiguous to the Kyles, appear much more dark. I came in upon Loch Carron at the narrowest place, nigh where it opens to the sea, when there was a boat just coming to land, freighted from a house several miles up on the other side of the loch, by some people bound to the place from whence I came. I waited their arrival, thinking it a good chance, but in this I was mistaken. No arguments would persuade them to take me along with them. They alleged that it was depriving the ferryman of his right. But effectually to remove this impediment, I offered them triple freight, but they dared not to trust themselves with such a sum, for they actually rowed off, and left me standing on the rocks, where I was obliged to bellow and wave my hat for no small space of time. The ferryman charged sixpence and *a dram of whisky*. I then kept the North-west side of the loch, which stretcheth about ten miles into the country, following a kind of formed road; but on which a wheeled carriage seemed never to have gone, nor had the makers ever intended that it should.

The hills on each side of the lake are of a moderate height, but rise much higher as you advance into the country. The arable land was confined to very narrow limits, consisting of great numbers of small detached spots. I was exceedingly gratified at here meeting with a long, straggling village, consisting wholly of neat, modern, commodious houses. Having never heard of it, I made enquiry concerning its erection, and was informed that it had lately arisen under the auspices of Mackenzie of Applecross, who had let it off in feus to the fishermen, and such as chose to settle there. This is a most laudable example set by this gentleman, an example of which every reflecting mind must approve, and which can never be too much encouraged, either by individuals or by public bodies of men. It is only by concentrating these hardy and determined people into such bodies, that they shall ever be enabled to acquire the proper benefit of the inestimable fishings on their coasts, or that ever the germs of manufactures shall be succesfully planted on these distant shores.

This spot pitched on by Applecross for so beneficial a purpose is not so commodious in every respect as it might be wished that it were; but perhaps Applecross had no better. In this spot it is impossible to unite utility with compactness and elegance, for there being no valley the houses are drawn out in an irregular line along the side of the loch, and however well situated for taking advantage of trade and fishing, it is a very intoward field for improvements in agriculture.

Passing on, I went past the church, and through a carse, reaching New Kelso to my breakfast, a distance of nearly twenty miles from Ardhill. This is a spacious house, with a well-stocked garden for such a soil. It stands in the middle of a large, coarse plain, a great part of which is uncultivated, and which could only be cultivated with much labour. The history of the erection of this place by Mr. Jeffrey, and for what purpose, is too well known to need recapitulation here.

Proceeding up the glen, I lost sight of Loch Carron, crossed a rapid river which issued from amongst the hills to the north, saw numbers of Highland cottages in clusters, sheep, mostly of the old Highland breed, and some goats, and at last came to a change-house, of which I do not know the name, at the north-east corner of a lake in the middle of the Strath. I recognised it as such by a half-mutchkin pot that stood on the window. I entered, and called for a dram and some meat. The dram was understood, and a half-muthkin of good whisky brought to me (they do not deal in gills hereabouts), but no meat. I understood that the master and mistress were both absent at some place of worship, as no one ever appeared to me but two girls, who were visibly menials. I again called, and ordered some meat. A girl answered me in Gaelic, and I her in English, for a good while without either of us being the wiser. I then made signs to let her know that I wanted meat, taking care to give the whisky a push that she might not think that I wanted some more of it; but, in spite of my teeth, I was misconstructed, and another half-mutchkin of whisky clapped down to me in another pot. I expostulated a great deal; to no purpose. The girls came both into the room, and being tickled by our embarrassment, opened the flood-gates of their mirth, giggling and laughing aloud. I was inflamed by one of those sudden bursts of passion which sometime, although not very frequently, quite overcome my reason. Springing up in a rage, and swearing like a trooper, I laid hold of them violently, and turned first the one, and then the other, out of the room, and closing the door behing them with a force as if I were wished to throw down the house; while the poor creatures were so affrighted that their limbs almost refused their office of furthering their escape, the girls thinking, I daresay, that they were attacked, and their master's house taken up by a ruffian.

I threw myself again into my seat over my whisky, where in less than a minute I began to repent most heartily of my folly. Never did I yet suffer myself to get into a rage but the reflection cost me dear.

I would willingly have tarried a night hereabout, thinking it a country about the state of which it was worth my while to make some inquiry; but judging it impossible to lodge here, I again called *ben* one of the maids who entered with great caution, and with the most timid air imaginable. I assumed as mild a demeanour as I was able, offering her what money she thought proper to accept of. Seeing one of the stoups untouched, she charged sixpence.

I again took to my road. I began to grow very impatient, knowing that it would infallibly lead me into the country where I had been last year, and at length, seeing a small, winding, path ascending the mountains to the northward, I took to it without hesitation. But as my letters are always growing longer I will leave off.

James Hogg

Letterewe
Monday 13th June

Dear Sir, — I took an abrupt leave of you in my last, while climbing the mountains and just about to take my last look of the country of Loch Carron.

I must here explain a circumstance to you which I believe I have never done yet, and which I ought to have done long ago, that is, what is meant by *a country* in the Highlands. In all the inland glens the boundaries of a country are invariably marked out by the skirts of the visible horizon as viewed from the bottom of the valley. All beyond that is denominated *another country,* and is called by another name. It is thus that the Highland countries are almost innumerable. But on the western coast, which is all indented by extensive arms of the sea, and where the countries that are not really islands, are peninsulas, the above usage is varied, and the bounds of the country marked out by the sea coast. Along the whole of the shores of Argyll and Inverness shires, this latter is the division, but as soon as you enter Rosshire, the former is again adopted. Thus the country of Kintail, the country of Loch Carron, the country of Torridan, the two straths of Loch Broom, etc., comprehend both sides of their respective firths, with all the waters that descend into them.

Shortly after I lost sight of the valley my path divided into twain, equally well frequented. I hesitated long which to take, having no directions saving what I had from the map, but following the left hand one it led me at length into the Vale of Colan, a curious, sequestered place, in the midst of the mountains to the cast of Sir Hector Mackenzie's forest. The haughs are of considerable extent, of a deep sandy soil, with a clear stream winding through them; and some of the haughs were very good for such a country. The hills around it were very black, and mostly covered with strong heather.

I spoke to no person here, nor all this way, but again took to the muir, being resolved if possible to reach the house of Letterewe that night, but ere I got into the next valley I was quite exhausted by hunger and fatigue, having travelled an unconscionable length of way, and a slated house appearing on a plain beyond the river I made toward it.

I was obliged to wade through the river once, which being in a swelled state was very deep, and getting to the house asked if it was an inn, and was answered in the affirmative, at which I was very well satisfied. At this place I lodged. It is called Kinlochewe; was built by Sir Hector Mackenzie, in order to accommodate himself and others travelling from Dingwall into his country of Gairloch, or toward the ferry of Poolewe, where there is a packet once each week to Lewis, and though he hath several advantages to it, it is very ill kept and in very bad order. He had only a few days preceding that, lodged there himself, and had certainly little reason to pleased with accommodation. The floor was well sanded as is the custom in that country. The windows were broken, and the bed was as hard as stone. They had however plenty of whisky, oat-meal cakes, tea, and sugar, with some eggs, and stinking fish, on which I fared sumptuously.

I spent the following forenoon in the company of a Mr. Mackenzie, a farmer in a glen above that. He conducted me along a part of the road to Letterewe, and showed me the old burying ground of Ellon Mare, on the gravestones of which no name nor epitaph is to be seen, saving one or two rude figures and some initials.

I at length arrived at the house of Letterewe, and was received by Mr. M'Intyre (to whom I was recommended by a friend) with much kindness without any ceremony. This was exactly a man for my purpose. He had been from his youth an extensive dealer, both in cattle and sheep, and had travelled over the whole Highlands and Western Islands, and now in company with some English gentlemen farms an extraordinary extent of land, consisting of the whole estates of Letterewe and Strathnashalloch, the former belonging to Mr. Mackenzie, to whose sister he is married, and the other to Mr. Davidson.

He hath a handsome house and offices, which he, however, is going to enlarge, and having discovered large veins of white marble up in the linns of a rivulet near the house, he burneth it into lime, using it both for building and manure, and manageth the croft lying around his house in a manner which would not disgrace the banks of the Forth. There were to be seen shotts of turnips and potatoes, in drills as straight as a line, and in a forward state of vegetation, and clover and rye-grass so strong that it was beginning to lodge on the ground. The vigilance of the man is remarkable. This piece of land was one continued cairn of stones. Also the attention he pays to every department of his numerous flocks and shepherds is the most exact and constant, and he hath, by his vigilance and attention raised himself, from nothing, to affluence and credit. I had often heard of the man before I saw him. He was known on all the northern roads and markets by the appellation of *little Mackintyre*, he being low of stature, but as mettled at climbing among the rocks as the foxes — his greatest enemies.

As I am not in an humour for writing to-day, I shall close this letter with an anecdote of him which I had often heard told by Mr. James Welch.

The Hon. Lord Macdonald once at a market recognised the cattle from his farms in M'Intyre's possession, and began enquiring where he got them, who he got them from, etc. He informed his lordship in an indifferent manner, that he got them from Lord Macdonald's factor in Skye. But when the other began enquiring about the prices, and expenses, M'Intyre ignorant of who he was took him off so sharply that he knew not what to say excusing his curiosity, when a gentleman accompanying him introduced them to one another by their names. M'Intyre started, and with great quickness whipped of his bonnet, threw it on the ground, and placed his foot upon it, making an apology which pleased his lordship so much that he shook him by the hand, declaring that he was no stranger to his honesty, and adding, that the M'Intyres and the Macdonalds were the same people. I am, yours for ever,

James Hogg

Letterewe
Thursday, 16th June

Dear Sir, — I had conducted you in idea as far as Letterewe on the north-east bank of Loch Maree, and given you some hints of improvements commenced there by the farmer, which are only rendered remarkable by reflecting on the situation of the place.

It is, as I said, on the side of Loch Maree, by which there is access in boats from all corners of the lake, but it is everwhere else surrounded by shaggy cliffs, and bold, projecting promontories washed around the bottom by the lake, rising to the height of from one to four hundred yards, in an almost perpendicular direction. It is thus rendered inaccessible to the most expert foot passenger without a guide, and entirely so to horses, unless some passage is explored through amongst the mountains, that I never saw.

I proposed going to Ardlair next day, but was detained by the importunities of Mr. Mackintyre until the morning of the third day. He showed me everything in the vicinity that was worth seeing, and seemed much attached to me, being seldom visited by any from so distant a country.

There was another traveller wind-bound here, of a different description. This was Miss Jane Downie, sister to Mr. Downie, whose house I had lately left, who, from her father's house at the Manse of Urray, in the vicinity of Dingwall, was on a journey to the island of Lewis, to see some relations. Being daughter to a respectable clergyman, she had received a genteel education, a circumstance to which the utmost attention is paid by all families of rank in the north. To this she added an extensive knowledge of the world, of which she had seen a considerable part for one of her age and sex, for besides her acquaintance with both the Highlands and Lowlands, she had resided some years at St. Petersburgh with a sister, who was there distinguished by royal favour and protection.

It was this young lady who first inspired me with the resolution of visiting the remote country of the Lewis, by describing it to me as the scene of the most original and hereditary modes and customs that were anywhere to be met with in the British Isles.

On Wednesday we breakfasted early, and set off for Ardlair in Mr. Mackintyre's boat, who still insisted on our staying, assuring me that we would find much difficulty in our passage, if it was at all possible, the wind being so strong, and straight ahead. We had not proceeded far on the lake before we found this verified, and after rowing stoutly for about an hour, in which time we had not advanced a mile and a half, they put the boat ashore on the lee side of a point, declaring that it was impossible to proceed farther.

We were now much worse than if we had set off on foot from Letterewe. However, taking two men with us as guides, we *set a stout heart to a strait brae*, and explored a crooked way amongst the rocks; continuing for a long space to climb the hill in quite a contrary direction from the place we were bound to.

Our guides then led us over rocks and precipices, which on

looking at I thought a goat could not have kept its feet on, and had it not been owing to the nature of the stones, the surface of which was rough and crusty, it was impossible that we could have effected an escape, especially on such a day. I was in the greatest distress on account of the lady. The wind which had grown extremely rough took such impression on her clothes, that I was really apprehensive that it would carry her off, and looked back several times with terror for fear that I should see her flying headlong toward the lake like a swan.

It was however a scene worthy of these regions, to see a lady of a most delicate form and elegantly dressed, in such a situation, climbing over the dizzy precipices in a retrograde direction, and after fixing one foot, hanging by both hands until she could find a small hold for the other. What would the most of your Edinburgh ladies have done here, my dear sir? I believe if the wind had not changed they might have stayed with little Mackintyre altogether, for they could not have passed over these rocks.

Miss Downie's clothes were partly torn and otherwise abused, and the wind carried off her kerchief altogether. For upwards of a mile we were forced to scramble in this manner, making use of all fours, and in one place I was myself afraid of growing giddy, and durst not turn my eyes toward the lake so far below my feet. We, however, arrived safe at Ardlair at one o'clock, p.m., having been *five hours* on our passage, which in distance would not measure as many English miles, and were received by the Messrs. Mackenzie with great politeness and attention, and we soon became extremely happy, and though we did not forget, laughed most heartily at our late perilous situation.

The weather growing more moderate toward the evening we made a most agreeable excursion round several of the principal islands of Loch Maree in a handsome boat with a sail. These islands have a much more bare appearance than they exhibited some years ago, the ancient woods with which they were covered being either entirely cut down and removed, or most miserably thinned. One island on which there are some remains of a temporary residence is covered with wood and rich verdure. We landed on several of them and carried off numbers of eggs from the nests of the gulls, thousands of which were hovering and screaming around us. The Holy Island was so far to the leeward that we could not visit it that night for fear we should not get back.

I was truly delighted with the view from these islands, although it consisted much more of the sublime than of the beautiful. The old high house of Ardlair faced us from a romantic little elevated plain, bounded on the north with a long ridge of perpendicular rock of a brown colour, and the low islands on which we stood were finely contrasted with the precipitous shores already mentioned, on the one side, and the mountains of Sir Hector Mackenzie's forest on the other, whose pointed tops bored the firmament, and appeared of a colour as white as the finest marble.

I was greatly pleased with the Mackenzies, as well as with the old lady of Letterewe, their mother, (the gentlemen present being brethren to the proprietor,) and began to think that the farther north I proceeded I was still going to find the people more intelligent, and possessing qualities more and more estimable. As I had a line of introduction to Mr. John, the youngest, from a friend in Edinburgh, he furnished me with one to an acquaintance in the Lewis.

Next morning we arose and departed. Mr. Alexander Mackenzie of Auchnasheen (towards Woodrigill), one of his farms on which his family resides, and Mr. John and I, again entered the boat, and having a fair wind we skipped along the surface of Loch Maree with great velocity. We landed on St. Mary's Isle, and I had the superstition to go and drink of the holy well so renowned in that country among the vulgar and superstitious, like me, for the cure of insanity in all its stages, and so well authenticated are the facts, the most stubborn of all proofs, that even people of the most polite and modern ways of thinking, are obliged to allow of its efficacy in some instances. But as mine was only an attack of poetical hydrophobia, including my tendency to knight errantry, which however ridiculous to some, I take pleasure in. I omitted, however, the appendage of the ceremony, which in all probability is the most necessary and efficacious branch of it, namely, that of being plunged over head and ears three times in the lake.

But although I write thus lightly to you of the subject, I acknowledge that I felt a kind of awe on my mind on wandering over the burying-ground and ruins of the Virgin's chapel, held in such veneration by the devout, though illiterate fathers of the present generation. This I mentioned to Mr. Mackenzie, who assured me that had I visited it before the wood was cut down, such was the effect, that it would have been impossible not to be struck with a religious awe.

Shortly after we arrived again at Letterewe, where I took leave of you in my last, and where your fancy must leave me until my next arrival, until when

I remain, sir, your most affectionate servant,

Dundonnel
Thursday 16th June

Dear Sir, — Leaving the banks of Loch Maree, I mounted the hills of Letterewe, accompanied by Mackintyre and Mackenzie, who, perceiving that my attention was much taken by the uncouth scenery, promised that they would lead me through some which I should not see equalled in Scotland, and I believe they were as good as their word, the whole scenery in some parts of Letterewe estate being dreadful and grand beyond measure; and here, as in places of that nature throughout the Highlands, the principal parts were named after some of the Fingalian heroes. The lake is named after the chief, being denominated Loch Fion, or the Fion Loch.

To enumerate particularly the different appearances of each tremendous precipice that interlards this truly terrific scene is impossible. I neither have time nor words suited to the description, but I cannot avoid taking notice of the black rock, or Craigtullich; for although any other of these views may be matched in the country, yet this one is certainly not only unequalled, but far out of reach of comparison. It extends a whole English mile in length, along all which extent there is not a passage where a creature could not pass, and it is so appropriately termed black that it appears wholly stained with ink, and its dreadful face, all of which can be seen from one view, everywhere distorted by dark slits, gaping and yawning chasms, with every feature of a most awful deformity, conveying to the attentive spectator ideas of horror which could scarcely be excelled by a glimpse of hell itself!

Should a merry companion choose, in order to enjoy the sight of the most profound and exquisite tumble, to give you an unmannerly push from the top of it, you might descend for nearly half a mile in the most straight line towards the centre of gravity. You might indeed happen to leave a rag of your coat on the point of one cliff, or a shoe, or your brains perhaps on another, but these are trifling circumstances. The worst thing attending it would be, that the pleasure arising from a view of your gracefully alighting would be entirely lost from the top, as you would appear of no greater magnitude than a forked bulrush. Remember that it is your fancy that I am addressing myself, my dear sir. I always wish you to see everything nearly the same as I did.

At a great distance he showed me a large perpendicular rock, with the entrance to a cavern near the bottom. In this dismal hole, in the midst of this huge wilderness, wonderful to relate, a widow and her family hath resided many years! When she first took possession of this dreary abode her youngest son was a sucking infant. Yet she was obliged to cross the mountains once a week to seek milk and other articles of food; while owing to their being so inaccessible she was unable to carry her child along with her, and was obliged to put out the fire and leave him to shift for himself. He had by such lodging and treatment acquired a weakness in his back, and it was feared he would never overcome it, as he still could not walk, but only creep, though I think they said he was six or seven years of age.

Mr. Mackenzie told me that he was once passing that way with an English gentleman, on business in that country, and observing no smoke, he suspected the woman to be from home, so without mentioning anything of the matter to his companion he led him to take a view of the cavern. The gentleman was almost out of his wits when he saw a creature bearing such a resemblance to the human form, come crawling towards him from the interior of the cavern. Alas! my dear Sir, one half of the world knows little how the other half lives. 'Nor how they die either, James,' you will add when you read the following.

In a deep sequestered hollow among these rocks, my friend showed us a shealing far beneath our feet, where a man and his wife lately came to reside during the summer months with their cattle and goats. The woman fell a travailling in childbirth, and for want of assistance, which was impossible there to be procured, there she died and was buried.

From a precipice near to this we had a view of a curious bason of very romantic dimensions, but in order to see it properly we were obliged to lie down full length on our breasts, and make long necks over the verge. I was afraid to trust my head, and ordered Mr. Mackenzie to keep a firm hold of the tails of my coat, but before I could reach so far as to have a proper survey, I was obliged to roar out to be pulled back, my 'conscience having failed me,' as I once heard a boy say in the same predicament.

We proceeded on in company through a large track of this rough country, and were often so immersed among rocks, that I saw no possibility of escaping, but Mackintyre was so well acquainted with the gaps that he always found an open door, as he termed it. Nor did they ever leave me until they landed me in one of the glens of Strathinashalloch, having conducted me full ten miles, and I took leave of them deeply impressed with their kindness and attention. I shall have occasion to take notice of some intelligence received from Mackintyre afterwards.

I now proceeded down a glen several miles in length, which brought me into the Valley of Strathinashalloch, near the head of the lake of that name. The valley is now inhabited only by Mr. MacKintyre's shepherds, but there were considerable crops of corn and potatoes left by the tenants who had removed last term. It is of considerable extent, and there is good fishing in the river and loch, which is entirely free. This estate is now the property of Mr Davidson, and though there are some more detached parts arable, and possessed by the natives, the greatest extent is now farmed by Mr. Macintyre, at the trifling rent of £200; and I am certain, if things continue at present prices, that he may have a clear return of £600 or £700 a year from it, if once he had a proper stock on it, which he had not when I saw it, having only entered at Whitsunday.

He showed me the boundary on one side, and his shepherd the same on the other, and I could not compute that part held by him alone at less than 15,000 acres, all of which is well mixed, good Highland ground, most of it accessible, not being nearly so rough as Letterewe; free of lying stones, and tolerably well sheltered. What an excellent bargain at such a time!

The truth is, there are several low-country gentlemen getting into excellent bargains by their buying lands in that country, of which Mr. Davidson and Mr. Innes are instances; and I cannot help having a desperate ill-will at them on that score. I cannot endure to hear of a Highland chieftain selling his patrimonial property, the cause of which misfortune I always attribute to the goodness of his heart, and the liberty of his sentiments; unwilling to drive off the people who have so long looked to him as their protector, yet whose system of farming cannot furnish them with the means of paying him one-fourth, and in some situations not more than a tenth of the value of his land; and as unwilling to let fall the dignity of his house, and the consequence amongst his friends, which his fathers maintained. Is not his case particularly hard, my dear sir? All things are doubled and tripled in their value, save his lands. His family — his retainers — his public burdens! These last being regulated by the old valuation, lie very hard upon him, and all must be scraped up among the poor, meagre tenants, in twos and threes of *silly* lambs, hens, and pounds of butter.

I shall follow the idea no farther else I shall run mad, but as the value of these hills is every year more and more conspicuous, I anticipate with joy the approaching period when the stigmas of poverty and pride so liberally bestowed on the highlanders by our south-country gentry will be as inapplicable to the inhabitants of that country as of any in the island. Their riches are increasing, and will increase much more, and when that shall be the case they will require no pride, as that has mostly consisted in maintaining the appearance of a rank to which in reality their circumstances were quite inadequate.

After going over another track of bare rocky land I descended the beautiful strath of little Loch Broom, and before sunset arrived at the house of Dundonnel, the seat of George Mackenzie, Esquire, of Dundonnel.

I am, yours, etc.

James Hogg

"Isabella" Loch Broom
Monday 20th June

Dear Sir, — I was received by Dundonnel at the head of the green before the house, he having, it seems, eyed my approach from one of the windows, and he welcomed and introduced me to his family with a respectful attention and ceremony which greatly distressed me; and notwithstanding every endeavour at a more unreserved familiarity, it rather increased than diminished during my stay. Every time that I entered the room, the whole family, small and great, must be on their feet to receive me, so that in spite of Dundonnel's good humour, and he is a remarkably cheerful and unassuming man, I was in no wise easy, on account of the stir that I occasioned in the family, and the rich meals that were provided.

He hath one master for instructing his family in the languages, and arithmetic; and another for teaching them music and dancing. We had thus plenty of music at night, having always three fiddles in tune; and every one bore a hand at swelling the lively concert, where the Highland strathspeys and reels were the prevailing strains. They were pleased to applaud my performance, which caused me to saw away as if I had it by the piece.

We always remained at the punch-bowl until the blackbird sung at the window, as this was Dundonnel's rule, which custom he would not dispense with. We spent a day in viewing the strath, and to have a better general view of the estate Mr. George and I climbed to the top of a hill on the ridge betwixt the two loch-Brooms. It extends fully eighteen Scotch miles from east to west, and may be about ten miles broad, at an average, but on the south it is terribly interwoven with Mr. Davidson's ground. It is an excellent pastoral estate, and the vale of the little strath is pleasant and fertile. It hath plenty of natural wood in its upper parts, and the laird hath beautified the vicinity of his mansion-house with extensive plantations, which are in a thriving state.

Most of the reflections in my last may be applied to Dundonnel. His glens are so crammed full of stout, able-bodied men and women, that the estate under the present system must have enough to do maintaining them. The valleys are impoverished by perpetual cropping, and saving one farm on the northeast quarter, held by the Messrs. Mitchell, the extensive mountains are all waste; for the small parcels of diminutive sheep which the natives have, are all herded below nearest the dwellings, and are housed every night. Dundonnel asked me what I thought it would bring annually if let off in sheep walks. I said I had only had a superficial view of it, but that, exclusive of a reasonable extent near the house, to be occupied by himself, it would bring not below £2,000. He said his people would never pay him the half of that. He was loath to chase them all away to America, but at present they did not pay him above £700. He hath, however, the pleasure of absolute sway. He is even more so in his domains than Bonaparte is in France. I saw him call two men from their labour a full mile, to carry us through the water. I told him he must not expect to be served thus by the shepherds if once he had given them possession.

I now understand on enquiry that I must either relinquish my visit to the Lewis, or to Sutherland, for that there was no possibility of obtaining a passage. After leaving Ullapool, and learning on the third day after my arrival at Dundonnel, that the *Isabella* of Stornoway had been taking in a load of stones on the south shore of Loch Broom, and was only waiting the arrival of one of the crew from the country, to set sail for that port, I took leave of Dundonnel, and set off in order to procure a passage by that vessel. I reached the place by two o'clock, but owing to a contrary wind, and the flow of the tide, they could not sail that night. I knew not what to do then. The crew were out of provisions, and there were none to be had in that place. There was a whole village of Highland cottages hard by, but when the sailors, who could talk Gaelic, could procure no provisions, by what means was I, who had no Gaelic, to support myself! As I was under the necessity of trying what could be done I went to all the houses, but could not get one word of English. There was, it seems, only one man amongst them who made the smallest pretensions towards it, and he being gone a little from home, some of them had the goodness to fetch him. He was the worst talker of English that I ever heard attempt it. It was downright nonsense, a mixture which no man could comprehend. He took me to his little hovel, and gave me whey to drink, but he had no bread until he baked it, which he made shift to do in the most unfeasible manner imaginable.

On parting with Dundonnel he said that if I wanted to be well treated on my passage to the Lewis, or yet to be welcome when I got there, I must necessarily pretend to want either horses or cows. I made some objections which he quite over-ruled, and I promised to obey; and on this man asking what I was wanting in that country I told him I wanted horses. Unluckily for me the man had horses to sell, and led me many miles out to the hills to look at them, and I could not get quit of buying them on account until I had to promise to come back that way and buy all the horses in the country, and on that day twenty days he was to have all the horses in the strath collected. I was heartily tired of Dundonnel's plan, and fully convinced of the justness of the old proverb, 'truth tells aye best'. I trust that never more in the course of my journey shall I have recourse to equivocation. The man had no one in the house with him saving a child of four years old. I asked 'What had become of his wife?' His answer was, 'He pe con see hir muter; he pe shild lenoch after her.' There were some of his horses which he denominated *girrons*, others were *pullocks*, and some were *no pullocks*. He had no milk in his house, only some sour whey, the cows being out on the hills at the shealings. He made sowens to our supper, but as he did not use the necessary precaution to shill, or strain them, they were unconsciously rough with seeds.

I now began to look about me where I should sleep, but he did not long suffer me to remain in suspense, for bringing in a large arm-full of green heather, he flung it down by the side of the wall, then strewing a few rushes over it, he spread one pair of clean blankets over it, and there was my bed. I found fault with nothing, but stripping to the skin, I wrapped myself first in my shepherd's plaid, and then covered me with his blanket. I made shift to pass the night, although not very agreeably, for, as the tops of the heather depressed, the stubborn roots found means more and more to annoy my shoulders and ribs, and so audacious were some of them that they penetrated Donald's white blanket, and I left them so firmly connected, that I am sure on his removing the blanket, a good many of the roots would adhere to it.

Yesterday morning I came on board the sloop, and about seven o'clock a.m., we heaved anchor and got under way, but as the small breeze that was blowing was straight ahead of the vessel, we beat up the whole day without getting out of the loch, sometimes among the Summer Isles, and sometimes hard off the shore opposite them, to the south, and at the close of the day we found ourselves immediately off a rocky point betwixt the channel and the broad loch. Here the boat was sent ashore to bring a lady on board, who was bound to Stornoway. She was not ready, and the master of the vessel was obliged to wait on her, she being mother of the owner. There being no anchorage nigh, he was forced to lie to in the entrance all night, in the worst humour that possibly could be, cursing the whole sex, and wishing them all wind-bound for a season, and especially the old, weather beaten hulk, who caused him to endanger so good a vessel off the face of a rock, while the wind was sunk and the tide so violent.

As the sea was heavy in the mouth of the bay, the vessel wrought incessantly during the whole night. I became very uneasy, but knowing nothing of the nature of the sea fever, I thought I was attacked by the influenza, but how was I vexed this morning at having suffered such a night, when I was shown the house of Woodrigill, at the end of a bay not an hour's walking distant, where I could have lodged with the kind Achnasheen. I remain, your most obedient,

"Isabella" The Minch
Wednesday 22nd June

Sir, — I took leave of you in my last while lying on board, sick of the influenza; but having got no meat for a whole natural day,

104

saving a small piece of cake and a little old cheese, I was becoming extremely hungry, and desired two of the crew to row me ashore. I went to the house of Melton, and took a hearty breakfast with Mrs. Morrison, who immediately after accompanied me to the vessel, and we began to steer onward, but the breeze continuing straight ahead, it was near noon before we got into the open channel.

As soon as we got clear of the Summer Isles, the tide then turning to the north, we took a long stretch in the same direction, passed the Summer Isles, doubled the point of Coygarch, and the day being fair and clear, got an excellent view of the mountains of that country. They had a verdant appearance, but a passenger assured me that the fine weather made them appear so, for that they were nevertheless mostly covered with a mossy surface.

Still holding on in the same direction, and having an excellent spy-glass on board, we got a view of the shores of Loch Eynard; and passing the Rhu of Assynt, although then at a considerable distance out on the channel, a prodigious range of the rugged mountains on Lord Reay's country presented itself to view, forming the most striking and perforated outline I had yet seen. I was afterwards convinced that the extraordinary appearance which they exhibited had been occasioned in part by some small skiffs of mist which had been hovering about their summits, and which I had taken for the horizon beyond them, these causing them to appear as if bored through in many places.

Our skipper steered thus far to the north in hopes that the breeze would drop into the north-east before evening. In this, however, he was disappointed, and the tide turning to the south, he tacked about, steering to the south-west, or a little to the west, and a little before sunset the breeze sunk entirely, and there was not a breath. My patience now took its leave of me for some time altogether. Although I was never actually sick, yet I found myself growing squeamish and uneasy, forsaken by the breeze in the very midst of a broad channel, and, for anything that I knew, condemned to hobble on that unstable element for a week, or perhaps much longer.

Mrs. Morison, who is well versed in naval affairs, and has been frequently known to take the helm into her own hand in dangers, perceiving my face growing long, gave me a dram, and expressed her surprise that I was no worse, having never been at sea before, assuring me that a calm was worse to endure than a gale.

As the sails continued all set, waiting to take advantage of the first breeze, and as they flapped and wrought in conjunction with the waves, the ship rolled exceedingly at times. I, who imputed no part of it to the rigging, could not forbear, in my then desperate condition, from expressing, with great bitterness and folly, my indignation at the malevolence of the sea, that would not be still and at peace, when nothing was troubling it, asking the sailors 'What was putting it astir now when there was not a breath? It was certainly an earthquake.' There was, however, one comfort. We were in no danger now of perishing for hunger, Mrs. Morison having brought plenty on board from her farm. During the first day, when cruising in Loch Broom, the master and I were forced to content ourselves with a fardle cake between us, and a piece of old cheese, the sailors regaling themselves with some crabbed shell-fish and sea-weeds, which they had scraped from the rocks on shore. Highlandmen are not nice of their diet. But now we had plenty of tea, sugar, eggs, cakes, and fish.

My chagrin was somewhat diverted near the fall of evening by contemplating the extensive prospect. We were becalmed exactly in the middle of the channel which separates Lewis from the mainland, and the evening being remarkably fine and clear we could see distinctly the Isle of Skye, the Shant Isles, the Lewis, and all that range of mountains in Ross-shire and Sutherland, stretching from Torridon to Cape Wrath. By reason of their distance they now appeared low. The sea, though in its natural perturbed state, being unruffled by the smallest breeze appeared an ocean of heaving crystal, of different colors in different directions, presenting alternately spots of the deepest green, topaz, and purple; for which I could not in the least account by any appearance in the sky, which was all of one colour.

Such a scene, so entirely new to me could not fail of attracting my attention, which it did to such a degree that I remained on deck all night. The light of the moon at length prevailed. She hovered low above the Shant Isles, and shed a stream of light on the glassy surface of the sea, in the form of a tall crescent, of such lustre that it dazzled the sight. The whole scene tended to inspire the mind with serenity and awe, and in the contemplation of it I composed a few verses addressed to the Deity, which I will give you bye and bye, and if you apprehend that they move a little more heavily than my verses were wont to do, remember that they are *sea-sick*.

VERSES ADDRESSED TO THE DEITY.
Great source of perfection, and pole of devotion!
    Thy presence surrounds me wherever I roam;
  I see Thee as well in the wild heaving ocean
    As in the most sacred magnificent dome.
While viewing this scene with amazement and wonder,
    I see Thee in yonder moon's watery gleam.
Thy voice I have heard from the clouds burst in thunder;
    Now hear it from wild fowls which over me scream;
Oh! teach me to fear, to adore, and to love Thee
    As Sovereign of earth and those heavens I see.

But oh! above all, with warm gratitude move me
    For all Thy great mercies bestow'd upon me,
In all my lone wand'rings, oh guide and direct me,
    As round the bleak shores of the Hebrides I roam,
From evils and dangers defend and protect me,
    And lead me in peace to my sweet native home.
And when my life's wearisome journey is ended,
    May I, in Thy presence, those heavens survey,
So sanded with suns! amid seraphs so splendid
    To sing, where no night shall encroach on the day.

'Ay James; I never saw you in so serious a mood as this before.' ''Tis no matter my dear sir; I am very often in such a mood, but it never continues long at a time.'

During all this time, although we varied our position greatly to the North, and South, with the tides, we were quite stationary as to proceeding in our course, the vessel floating with her stern towards Stornoway. I wished myself fairly on terra firma again; I cared not on which side of the channel.

Early in the morning, all being quiet, I had wrapped myself in my shepherd's plaid, and was stretched among some cables on deck, busied in perusing Shakespeare's monstrous tragedy of 'Titus Andronicus,' and just when my feelings were wrought to the highest pitch of horror, I was alarmed by an uncommon noise, as of something bursting, and which I apprehended was straight over me, when starting up with great emotion, I was almost blinded by a shower of brine. But how was I petrified with amazement at seeing a huge monster, in size like a horse, sinking into the sea by the side of the vessel, something after the manner of a rope tumbler, and so near me that I could have struck him with a spear. I bawled out to the crew to be upon the alert, for that here was a *monstrous whale* to *coup* the ship, and seizing the boat-hook was going, as I thought, to maul him most terribly. He had rather got out of my reach, and one of the crew took it from me for fear I should lose it, assuring me that I could not pierce him although it was sharp, which it was not.

After the sun rose, the sails began to fill, and we moved on almost imperceptibly towards Stornoway. The whale kept by the vessel the whole morning; sometimes on one side, sometimes on the other. Being always immoderately addicted to fishing, I was in the highest degree interested. I was also impatient at such a huge fish being so near me. He was exactly the length of the vessel, a sloop, if I mistake not, about seventy or eighty tons. I once called to one of the sailors to come and see how he rubbed sides with the ship. 'Eh! said he, 'he pe wanting one of us to breakfast with him!' Your most obedient,

Ettrick Shepherd

107

Dear Sir, — We at length entered the harbour of Stornoway, and about seven o'clock in the evening cast anchor within a very short space of the houses, having been exactly sixty hours on the passage, a distance of scarcely so many miles.

As soon as I arrived, I went to the head inn, held by Mr. Creighton, a silly, despicable man, but privileged in having an excellent wife. During the whole of that evening I could not walk without taking hold of everything that came in my way, impressed with an idea that all things were in motion. I was very unfortunate in not meeting with the people to whom I was recommended here. I had a letter for Mr. Chapman at Seaforth Lodge, but he was absent in Uig, parting some land, and Mrs. Chapman being in a poor state of health, I never presented myself. I had a letter to Mr. Donald Macdonald, and another to Mr. Robertson, both of Stornoway, and in whose company I spent some time; but the one was obliged to go from home in the packet, and the other did not come home until the last day that I was there.

I wandered about the town and neighbouring country for three days, sometimes in company with one, and sometimes with another. There is a Captain Marshall, from the neighbourhood of Fochabers, lodging in the same house with me, a sober, sensible man, with whom I was very happy.

I was indeed greatly surprised at meeting with such a large and populous town in such a remote and distant country. It was but the preceding week that I ever heard of it, and yet it is quite unrivalled in all the west of Scotland north of the Clyde, either in population, trade, or commerce. I was informed by Mr. Robison, comptroller of the Customs, that, according to the last survey, which was then newly taken, the town and suburbs contained nearly seventeen hundred souls. Mr. Macdonald, to whom I mentioned this, doubted its containing so many, but was certain that there were above a thousand.

There is one full half of the town composed of as elegant houses, with even more genteel inhabitants, than are generally to be met with in the towns of North Britain which depend solely on the fishing and trade. The principal and modern part of the town stands on a small point of land stretching into the harbour in the form of a T, and as you advance back from the shore the houses grow gradually worse. The poor people have a part by themselves, on a rising ground to the north-east of the town, and though all composed of the meanest huts it is laid out in streets and rows as regularly as a camp. The houses on the shore to the eastward and those at the head of the bay are of the medium sort. It hath an excellent harbour, and is much ornamented by the vicinity of Seaforth Lodge, which stands on a rising ground overlooking the town and harbour. The town is much incommoded by the want of streets or pavements. Even the most elegant houses facing the harbour, saving a small road close by the wall, have only the rough sea shore to pass and repass on, which being composed of rough stones, which fly from the foot, grinding on one another, forms a most uncomfortable footpath.

As the peculiarities observable in the modes and customs of the inhabitants are applicable to the whole island, I shall note a few of them on taking leave of it. I shall only observe here, that the well directed and attended schools, the enlightened heads, and enlarged ideas of a great number of the people of Stornoway bid fair to sow the seeds of emulation, and consequently of improvement in that remote country. It is a general complaint through all the Long Island that the poorer sort are much addicted to pilfering. I persuaded myself that I saw a striking evidence to the contrary in the inhabitants of this town. During the daytime there were thousands of white fish spread on the shores, drying on the sand. When night came they were gathered and built up in large heaps, and loosely covered with some coarse cloth, and when the sun grew warm next day were again spread. Now, my dear Sir, I'll wager you durst not have exposed your fish in such a manner at Edinburgh, for as fine a place as it is.

Although the island is not noted for riots, I had no very favourable specimen of their absolute command over their passions. On the very night of my arrival a desperate affray took place in the room adjoining to that in which I slept. Several respectable men, the collector, and one of the Bailiffs, were engaged in it. It was fought with great spirit and monstrous vociferation. Desperate wounds were given and received, the door was split in pieces, and twice some of the party entered my chamber. I was overpowered with sleep, having got none at sea, and minded them very little, but was informed of all by Mr. Marshall. A ship's captain, in particular, wrought terrible devastation. He ran foul of the table, although considerably to the windward, which he rendered a perfect wreck, sending all its precious cargo of crystal, china, etc. to the bottom, and attacked his opponents with such fury and resolution that he soon laid most of them sprawling on the deck. Some of the combatants being next day confined to their beds, summonses were issued, and a prosecution commenced, but the parties being very nearly connected a treaty was set on foot, and the preliminaries signed before I left Stornoway.

On the evening preceding my departure I hired a lad to accompany me round the island for eighteen pence per day, on condition that he was not to go off Lewis. At Creighton's the entertainment was as good as could be expected, for although they have neither brewer, baker, nor barber in the town, professionally, yet every man privileged with a beard is a barber, and every woman unencumbered with a family is a baker, and I suppose Mrs. Creighton is none of the most inferior practitioners, as we got very good wheaten loaves, though not exactly conformable in shape to those used in our country. Our breakfasts were thus rendered as comfortable as they are anywhere, and though at dinners and suppers we had seldom any beef or mutton, we had great abundance, as well as variety, of fish, fowls, and eggs. I expected my bill to run high, but how was I surprised on calling for it to see that I was charged no more than sixpence for each meal. I was agreeably deceived, and observed to my hostess that a man might eat himself rich here and fat at the same time. 'A very poor specimen of your wit, James!'

Thus being furnished with several letters, some whisky, biscuit, and a full half of a Lewis cheese, as hard as wood, Malcolm and I set out in the morning, and taking the only road in the whole island, proceeded northward through a dreary waste, without ever being blest with the sight of a human habitation, or a spot where it was possible to live upon, there being only one extensive morass the whole way. We passed a flock of native sheep, which was the greatest curiosity I had ever seen. I saw a man coming with hasty strides to waylay us. As I suspected that he would have no English I never regarded him, although he had got within speech as I passed, but Malcolm, who carried considerable weight, being fallen quite behind, he intercepted, and testified his regret that I had passed him, as he meant to treat us at his shealing.

Our road, after carrying us straight on for ten miles, like several of the Highland roads, left us all at once in the midst of a trackless morass, through which it had been cut at the deepness of several yards. The plan in making roads being mostly to clear the channel of whatever incumberance choke it up. Malcolm being now fallen at least a mile back I scorned to wait, but holding on in the same direction I soon discovered the northern ocean, and the manse of Barvas facing me at some distance, to which I bent my course, and reached it just as the family were rising from breakfast. I produced my letter of introduction, which the minister read, but declared it perfectly superfluous, for that my appearance was a sufficient introduction. I knew that this was to let me know how welcome a stranger was in that country, for alas! I knew that my appearance commanded no great respect. I was only dressed as a shepherd when I left Ettrick, and my dress was now become very shabby, and I often wondered at the attention shown me.

The Reverend Mr. Donald Macdonald seems to be a person in every way qualified for opening the eyes of an ignorant people to their real interests, both spiritual and temporal. His aspect and manner are firm and commanding, yet mixed with the greatest sweetness. Even when discoursing on the most common subjects, his style is animated, warm, and convincing. He is well versed in agriculture, and the management of different soils, which is of great importance in such a place; yet the people are so much prejudiced in favour of their ancient, uncouth modes, that but few follow his example. He is a Justice of the Peace, and is continually employed in distributing justice, for although the people are not much given to quarrelling or litigation, their rights in their farms are so confused and interwoven, that it is almost impossible to determine what share belongs to each. Supposing ten tenants possessing a farm, which is common enough, and every 'shot' or division of their arable land to consist of ten or more beds, or ridges, they do not take ridge about, and exchange yearly, nor yet part the produce, but every ridge is parted into as many subdivisions as there are tenants. Into tenths, twentieths, fourths, fifths, etc., every one managing and reaping his share, so that it would take a man to be master of fractions to be a tenant in Lewis. The pasture is regulated by the number of cattle, sheep, or horses, each possesses, and as there is no market for these save once a year, at the great tryste, some of the companies are often obliged to encroach on their neighbours' rights, or impose on their goodness. Thus it may well be supposed in what manner the ministers are harassed by continued applications for settling the most intricate differences.

There was a cause tried before Mr. Macdonald when I was there which lasted some hours, but it being conducted in Gaelic, I could only understand it by a general explanation. They submit, though sometimes reluctantly, to the decision of their pastor. From his court there are no appeals.

I am, sir, your ever faithful shepherd,

Barvas
Sunday 26th June

Dear Sir, — I took my leave of you at Barvas, near the Butt of the Lewis, where I arrived on one of the longest days of summer, and owing to the bright sky in the north, and the moon in the south, beaming on the ocean, *there was no night there.* Mr. Macdonald and I made an excursion along the shores of the northern ocean. The wind was indeed north-west, but the day was moderate, yet there was such a tremendous sea breaking against the shore as I never witnessed, nor indeed ever thought of before, there being no land to break it nearer than North America or Greenland. Every wave that came rolling against the perpendicular shore burst into the air as white as snow, to

111

the height of several hundred feet. There being no bays nor creeks on this coast where any vessel can anchor, what a dreadful sight it must present to mariners in a storm.

The sea having washed everything away but the solid rock, the shore is in many places perforated by extensive caverns which have never been explored. In one place near to Europa Point, or the Butt of the Lewis, of which we had a fine view, there is a subterraneous cavern across the land from one sea to the other. There is another in Uia which has been penetrated with lights to a distance of nearly a quarter of a mile, and in which are annually felled numbers of large seals. We likewise saw several insulated rocks along the shore, of considerable dimensions, and covered with sea fowls which hatch on them. Mr. Macdonald, who in his walks seems to delight much in contemplating their natural propensities, having little else to attract his notice, described several of their habits to me. The Solan goose, great numbers of which were continually passing, he described as the most persevering and indefatigable creature in search of its prey in the world, and adopting the most laborious means of obtaining it. It does not hover and watch over any certain place, but flies straight on over seas and oceans until some chance fish attracts its notice, when it immediately springs up to a great height in the air, and as near as he could judge, always to about the same height, from which he supposed they saw most distinctly, and then, after a few moments' pause taking aim, it darts down into the sea with inconceivable rapidity and force; and if it misses its prey, which must often happen, it again holds on its unwearied course. He described a method of taking them used by some of the fishers, which if not so well authenticated might be looked upon as fabulous. Well aware of the propensities of the Solan, they take a plank, in which they cut some apertures of a proper width. These they fix along with their nets, and leave them swimming on the surface, having a herring or other clear fish fixed to each of the apertures on the lower side. This catching the eye of the Solan goose, he, regardless of the intervening plank, dasheth his head into the hole, commonly with such force as to shatter his skull to pieces.

Mr. Mackenzie showed me a kind of sea-hawk, nearly as big as a Solan goose, the name of which in Gaelic signifies 'squeezer'. Whether properly applied, you may judge by the following description of its proceedings. It is of so vitiated a taste that it seems to depend wholly for subsistence on the excrement of the Solan geese, and as it is only in a certain stage that it is of use for it, it takes the following method of procuring this singular repast. It fixes upon one goose which it pursues without intermission, until it drops its excrement, which the squeezer hath the art to snatch at before it reacheth the water, and well satisfied with its alms, immediately quits that, and fixes upon another. Those that we saw of them were always in pursuit of geese.

The other things that we saw worthy of remark were the hills of sand contiguous to the manse. These are an insurmountable bar to improvement in that quarter, as a dry spring wind always opens them, and lays the whole of the crops of grass or corn adjacent, several feet deep in sand. These hills are accumulating from a sandy beach hard by, from which a strong north-west wind fetcheth immense loads of sand.

On the top of one of these hills is situated St. Mary's chapel, an ancient place of Popish worship. It had formerly been on the very summit of the eminence, but the sand is now heaped up to such a height as to be on a level with the gables. Yet the eddying winds have still kept it nearly clear, so that it appears as a building wholly sunk underground. The baptismal font is still standing in a place in the wall prepared for it. There are many of these in this parish, some of them of large and curious dimensions. There are also on its coasts some of the most entire Norwegian duns that are to be found in Scotland, the entrance to which is from the top. The purposes for which these were intended seem as much involved in obscurity as those of the pyramids of Egypt, to which they bear some resemblance. Mr. Macdonald also showed me a hill of small size from which he had seen sixty ploughs all going at a time. This will give you a very high idea of the fertility of the Lewis, or at least of the extent of the arable land there; and indeed this district of Ness, if it were not overstocked with people, and that it is under the most clumsy and untoward of all modes of cultivation, is certainly a *fertile place*, and is almost *wholly arable*, and composed of a variety of the richest soils, and what may seem remarkable, it enjoys the driest climate of the whole Western Highlands or Islands, as far as I could learn, even Islay not excepted.

This can only be accounted for by its lowness, there being no mountains of any height in the country. It occupies the northeast corner of the island, and Mr. Macdonald assured me that though in summer the showers came over the Atlantic as black as pitch, they always parted before they came there, one part flying towards the mountains and Lochs of Harris, and the others to the hills of Sutherland; so that while the hay and kelp were rotting in these countries, the people of the north parts of Lewis were often getting theirs winnowed with ordinary expedition. Also that when he first settled there, on seeing the clouds gathering on the Atlantic (for an approaching rain is seen at a great distance on the open sea), he would make a great hurry in getting his hay or corn put into a way in which it would receive least harm, disregarding the old people, who told him that he needed not make such a fuss, for that 'none of you would come near him'. Of the truth of this he was by degrees agree-

113

ably convinced.

The frosts in winter are never intense, the snow sometimes covers the ground to a considerable depth, but never continues long, and in places where ground is covered with a proper thickness of herbage, the cattle thrive very well lying out on it all the winter.

When the wind blows from any of the eastern quarters, the weather is commonly mild and dry. When from the western, hazy and accompanied with storms of wind and rain, and in the late years of scarcity, when the failure of the crop on the most fertile countries of Britain left the inhabitants almost starving, these islands never had so plentiful crops, either by land or sea, the fishing being equally favourable; and as the value of the cattle rose, they never experienced better times. But now, the case is for them sadly reversed; and whilst we are again swimming in plenty, they are perfectly reduced, by purchasing from other countries those necessaries of life which their own soil and bays have refused for the last two years to yield.

The people of this parish are industrious fishermen, and although their plans are the most simple, you will see by the papers that they always gain the most of the prizes held out by the society for dog-fish, cod, ling, and tusk. They have a terrible sea to fish on, and as terrible a shore to land upon. I could not avoid the old proverb, *'Rather them as me'*.

Yours sincerely,

James Hogg

West Lewis
Tuesday 28th June

Dear Sir, — Before I take my leave of Barvas it may not be improper to give you some idea of the mode of cultivation there, there being more arable land here than in any district of the Long Island, and a greater number of ploughs than in all the Long Island put together, for in this I reckon Ness included.

Their ploughs, numbers of which I saw, are very slender and shabby pieces of workmanship. They consist of crooked trees selected for the purpose. Through each of these a square hole is cut at the most crooked end, and here the stick that serves for the plough-head is fixed, and by wedging it above or below they give the plough more or less depth with great facility, as they give it less or more land by wedging it at the sides. Then almost straight above the heel a small stilt is fixed, and this is the plough. Although I saw several of their ploughs, not being there in the ploughing season, I have only seen two of them at work. A greater curiosity can hardly be exhibited to one who is a stranger to their customs. I could venture a wager that Cain himself had a more favourable method of tilling the ground. The man was walking by the side of the plough, and guiding it with his right hand. With the left he carried a plough-pattle over his shoulder, which he frequently heaved in a threatening manner at such of the horses as lagged behind; but as it had the same effect on them all, and rather caused the most fiery ones to rush on, he was obliged sometimes to throw it at the lazy ones. The coulter is very slender, points straight down, and is so placed that if it at all rip the ground it hath no effect in keeping the plough steady. The horses, impatient in their nature, go very fast, and the plough being so ticklish, the man is in a perpetual struggle, using every exertion to keep the plough in the ground, and after all, the furrow is in many places a mere scrape. The four ponies go all abreast, and such a long way before the plough, that at a little distance I could not imagine they had any connection with the man or it. They were all four tied to one pole, and a man, to whom the *puller* is a much more reliable name than the *driver,* keeps hold of it with both hands, and walking backwards as fast as he can, pulls them on. Those of them that walk too fast he claps the pole to their nose, which checks them. He finds means also to carry a small goad, with which he strikes the lazy ones on the face, asserting that that makes them spring forward. I had once an old brown mare, if he had struck her on the face he would have got her no farther in that direction. I can scarcely conceive a more disagreeable employment than that of this *'driver'* as he is called. The ploughman's post being such a very troublesome one he is mostly in a bad humour, and if the line of horses angle, the plough in spite of his teeth is pulled out of the land to the side on which the line is advanced. This puts him into a rage, and he immediately throws the pattle, or a stone at the hindmost. Now, although the man may be a tolerable good archer, yet passion may make him miss, and the driver runs a risk of meeting with the fate of Goliath of Gath. But granting that this should never happen, and the ploughman's aim should always hold good, yet 'I own 'tis past my comprehension' how a man can walk so fast the whole day in a retrograde direction without falling, (when he must that moment be trodden under foot by the horses). In fact I have seen many people who would be often missing their feet on such land although walking with their face foremost; and it is a fact that many of these drivers are hurt by accidents of the above nature. Upon the whole, a more improper method of tillage cannot well be conceived, as much of the ground is missed, that of it which is ploughed is rather crushed to one side than turned over, and as two of the horses are obliged to go constantly on the tilled land, it is by these means rendered as firm as before it was ploughed. You may perhaps think that I exaggerate in calling the district of Ness at the Butt of the Lewis *fertile,* but I am convinced that if the ground that I have had any concern with had been filled in the same manner, it would have produced crops much inferior, if any at all.

The natives are very industrious in gathering manure, and not inactive at making composts. They have one mode of procuring manure, which is, I think, peculiar to themselves. Their houses have very slender roofs, and are incapable of carrying a layer of divot or turf below the thatch, like the cottages in the south, but are merely covered with one light layer of straw or stubble, for instead of reaping, they pull their crops of barley wholly up by the roots, and those who are so fond as to adopt the foolish modern custom of reaping, have their stubble pulled up tightly after them. With this stuff the houses are thatched anew at the commencement of every summer, having been previously stripped to the bare rafters, and that which is taken off carefully spread upon the sand about the time when the crops begin to grow green. This is reckoned a valuable manure, and the land that it is spread upon commonly produceth a good crop, but they complain that it is a scourging one. The method of spreading this manure above is certainly injudicious, for being so well sharpened by the soot and smoke, it might enrich the soil considerably if buried in, or incorporated with it. But perhaps it would not be convenient to strip their houses so early.

I am sure you are now thinking it is high time that I were leaving Barvas. I beg your pardon, my dear sir, though I have kept you a good while there; Malcolm and I were not long there. We left it early this morning, stretching our course towards Loch Roag on the west coast of Lewis. We wandered on through trackless wastes, the whole of our course being through swamps and deep morasses, whilst our journey was constantly impeded by stagnant lakes, which, as the country was so flat, never appeared until we were hard upon them, casting widely off our aim. We are all the day uncertain where we shall land, but I feel much indifference, having letters for the principal men of each district. We saw great many sheep, goats, horses, and cattle, all straying at will on the muirs, and numbers of wild deer sprung from before us, and fled with great swiftness towards Ben Barvas. At length, growing hungry we sat down to eat some biscuit and cheese, which I told you before was as hard as wood. I now discovered that I had lost my pocket knife, and Malcolm had either lost his, or else he never had one; and in short, we found it impossible to get one bite of our cheese. Malcolm was despatched to a shealing, which was rather a covered cave, to borrow one. The inmates willingly sent the only one that they had, which was a piece of an old kelp-hook fixed in a deer's horn. This, instead of cutting our cheese, notwithstanding our utmost efforts, did not make the smallest impression. Malcolm was again despatched to a rivulet at a considerable distance, and came back carrying two large stones.

On one of these we laid the cheese, Malcolm sitting on his knees held it with one hand and the knife with the other, d—ning them both most heartily; whilst I with the other stone struck with all my force on the back of the knife. By these rude means we at length got it hacked into irregular pieces, and having allayed our hunger, and thirst, my dear Sir, we returned the knife, and shall proceed on our journey. But here I must again take my leave for a few days, protesting that I am at all times,

Yours sincerely,

Your most affectionate

James Hogg

1804

Dear Sir,

In addition to the tedious and uninteresting details which I have already transmitted to you of my journies through the Highlands, I must — I was going to say, crave your indulgence in perusing my third and last tour. This is however a matter of mere formality, and no very good form either; for if I were not within an ace of absolute certainty that the perusal would be productive of more sensible pleasure to you, than the writing of it is likely to procure me; and a thousand times more than my countrymen and I shall experience during the jaunt, of which I am about to attempt giving you the outlines, I would proceed no further; and the following word should be *last*.

Before I can proceed I must give you a sketch of the characters of each of my fellow travellers whom I shall distinguish by their christian names only. Mr. William, with whom I have been intimately acquainted from his childhood, was bred to the occupation of a farmer in the country, where he likewise received his education; and has no more experimental acquaintance with nautical affairs than proceeded from having once or twice gotten a view of the harbour, and arm of the sea. He has good natural parts, which he has, by reading, improved so far, as to have acquired a partial knowledge of most of the arts and sciences. He delights in painting, poetry, and music; is of a thoughtful disposition, absent, overbearing, and impatient of controul. Easily convinced by a single well-timed remonstrance, but immoveable by the most passionate and lengthened arguments. Mr. John, on the other hand, besides a good memory and judgement, has a mind extremely sensible to all the finer feelings: a taste for the sublime and beautiful, but rather too high-flavoured, to be generally good: enthusiastically fond of poetry and music, and no mean proficient in either: pays perhaps a little more deference to the opinions and temper of others than the former, but is ten times more impatient at being thwarted by contrary elements. From the habits of a town life, he has acquired ideas of the different degrees of mankind, and subordination of ranks, quite above what either Mr. W. or I have conception of; and thinks himself justly entitled to knock down every little d——d fellow or impertinent gipey of a girl, who does not answer a question or obey an order exactly to his mind, but withal possessed of an honest and generous heart. As for my own character, I leave that to be made out by you after perusing all these letters. But in short, we have all read of Fion Maccowl, and the maid of Colonsay; and have as much of the romantic in the disposition of our minds as, it equally divided, might have served other two, at least, of the same size with ourselves. I may likewise inform you, that I am at this time, obliged to visit the distant isle of Harries; and as all the Western Highlands and islands intervene, it was kindly agreed by these two young gentlemen to accompany me: and I dare say never any people set out with higher expectations of a most pleasing and delightful excursion. What romantic bays, and inchanted islands, have we in fancy already visited! what verdant pastures, vernal woods, and sweet blooming blushing maids! What pretty compliments have we already etched out as best suiting the illustrious highland chieftains at whose boards we should be quaffing the delicious nectar! I told you long ago my dear Sir, that *all is vanity*, and I cannot help here citing another piece of scripture, as better suiting our case than any note in Shakespeare that I remember just now, viz. "Let not him that putteth on his armour, boast like him that putteth it off."

Mr. William and I left Ettrick forest on the morning of the 21st of May 1804, having previously dispatched a letter to Mr. John, desiring him to meet us at Greenock. As we proposed walking, our travelling equipage was very simple. I had a small portmanteau, which we stuffed with each a clean shirt and change of stockings; a pocket travelling map, and a few neck-cloths. Thus nobly equipped, with each a staff in his hand, and a flashing tartan cloak over his shoulder, we proceeded on our enticing journey. We went over the dry mountains of Manor Water, crossed the Tweed at Dawick or New Passway the residence of Sir James Nasmyth; went through the village of Broughton, and in the evening reached the town of Biggar, situated in a high and damp climate, on the heights betwixt Tweedale and Clydesdale: having passed through a country, where the concerns of the husbandman are equally divided betwixt pasturage and tillage. The town is rather in a more flourishing state than might have been expected from its local advantages, the value of land in its immediate vicinity having of late increased with amazing rapidity. Leaving Biggar, we in short time time found ourselves on the banks of the Clyde; and proceeding by the two bridges, got a tolerable view of the country. It is a fine winding valley, but falls much short of the lower parts on the same river in natural beauty. It is however well stocked with an healthy and industrious peasantry, and there are few prospects, of any extent, in which the eye is not relieved by some handsome seat, where part of the surrounding policies are adorned by plantations of wood. As we approached Lanark these increased; and we noticed an extensive common capable of high improvement by cultivation, yet which is mostly quite neglected. We turned in to the left, in order to get a view

of the Cora linn, and at length reached it, not without much opposition from the gate-keepers. We saw it to a good advantage, the weather, being broken and rainy, and the river considerably flooded. It sends forth a deafening noise, which at times, borne on the breeze, assails at a great distance, the ear of the traveller, who looks in vain all around him for the rushing whirlwind, and is quite at a loss to what unknown cause in nature to ascribe the recurring phaenomenon.

The semicircular precipice, that surrounds the caldron to the north, is very grand; but as I expected the cascade to be much higher, it had no great effect upon me. On leaving it, after another quarrel at a gate, which we opened ourselves, we viewed the extensive cotton manufactory. This I am unable to describe to you, my notions with respect to machinery being very circumscribed, but it is certainly in a higher degree worthy of a visit, and of admiration too, than the Cora linn. We now entered the old useless burgh of Lanark, the *chief town* of that county in which Glasgow is situated, where we tarried a few hours. Certainly very few travellers must take Lanark in their way, for we could by no means attain any mode of travelling to Hamilton superior to that of walking. Not so much as a couple of horses could we have for hire in the whole town, altho' we should have been contented with any description of them. We again set out on foot: visited on our way the great fall of the Clyde adjoining the mill: these falls have been so often described, that no new thing can possibly be said about them; but I will wager a crown, that the miller, and all his people, may be distinguished in Lanark by their loud speaking; and farther, that if ever you shall see the cataract on Moffat-water, called the Grey-Mares-Tail, after a speat, you shall confess that the falls of the Clyde fall at least as much short of it, in awful sublimity, as I do Hercules. There was one thing I could not help noticing, that the water, on leaving these falls, appeared much more weak and powerless, than above them; and seemed, by them, to be broken and deprived of its natural solidity and force: but whether this reduction of the pristine strength of the water had any real foundation, or whether the change existed only in my brain, I have not philosophy enough certainly to discover. After this, the natural and artificial beauties of the Clyde lost much of their relish to us. The rain poured upon us in the most copious torrents, drenching us to the skin, and converting the road into a complete puddle; and though we professed a resolution of "splashing on thro' dub an' mire; despisin' wind an' rain an' fire," yet so easily is the contemplative faculty of the mind influenced by bodily sensation, that the serpentine windings of the Clyde, the delightful villas, the sweet ivy'd cottages, the numerous orchards loaden with blossoms, attracted no more

◁ Cora Linn

notice from us than perhaps a single look that way, or a point towards them with a foul end of a staff. About five o'clock afternoon we arrived at Hamilton, and lighting on good lodgings, and being desirous of seeing a little of the place; we tarried all night; and meeting with a fellow-traveller, spent the evening in the greatest glee. This morning we arose early, and spent the morning in viewing the policies around, and the paintings within Hamilton house: these are in the greatest variety, and executed by the greatest of masters. Till now I always flattered myself that I understood pictures tolerably well, and would give my opinion of the degrees of expression delineated in their looks with great readiness; but I here discovered, that I had no taste whatever, for though I joined with the rest in extolling Daniel amongst the lions, and some more old, ugly fellows, by Raphael, Titian, Vandyke, &c. I really found, that in my heart, I admired the parting of Hector and Andromache, and some modern pieces by Hamilton, much more. But finding that these did not suit the taste of my companions, whenever I saw a frightful, ill-looking figure, I praised that for its beauty, and never missed being joined by the rest, although, in fact, they were rather like hobgoblins than earthly creatures. Beauty is

one thing at an assembly, by dear Sir, and another in Hamilton house.

I am, Yours, &c.

James Hogg

Dear Sir, — I am, in these letters to you, always studying brevity, and as constantly running into the opposite extreme. I will be obliged to quit this epistolary way of communicating my sentiments to you altogether, as it hath no fixed boundary or limitation, and send you whole essays, or tours, in a parcel with the carrier.

In my last, I was got no farther than Hamilton, which is a neat elegant little town; and much beautified, as well as benefited, by the immediate vicinity of the mansion-house, and the attachment of the Dukes of Hamilton to the place from whence they draw their title. We set out in the mail coach at eight o'clock, and, in a short time, found ourselves at *the Saracen's Head,* in the city of Glasgow. This is a very cheap conveyance, being only two shillings inside, and the distance full nine miles. We flew too fast over this track for me to describe it particularly; for though we asked abundance of questions at the passengers, yet the quick succession of objects rendered it impossible for the memory to retain any traces so distinct as to be depended on.

It is true, we failed not to be continually pushing our heads out at the side-windows, and to pretend a deep interest in the appearance of the crops on the different soils; and were very attentive to impress upon others a deep sense of our importance and skill as farmers; and made many turn up the white o' th' eye to our discourse; who, if they had seen our own fields at home, would have been capitally convicted of the difference betwixt theory and practice. We also, very kindly, endeavoured to entertain our fellow travellers with appropriate remarks on the infallibility of the turnip husbandry succeeding to a miracle on such lands, and of its infinite superiority to their present modes of agriculture: unfortunately none of us could authenticate it, by an appeal to the abundant profits which we ourselves had reaped from that excellent plan.

At Glasgow, we tarried no longer than to breakfast, and call upon one of our countrymen; and the morning coaches being all gone, we took our passage for Greenock in the flyboat. It is not easy to conceive anything of the same nature more delightful than was our passage down the river that day. There was a brisk breeze from the south; the atmosphere was pure and light

after the rain, and objects discernible with perspicuity at a great distance; and tho' the vessel run with unusual velocity, yet, so smooth and steady was the motion, that we were obliged to call in the aids of philosophy to convince us that we were not quite stationary; and that the mountains, rocks, towns, and villages, were not all flying away like chaff before the wind.

We were landed safely on the quay at Greenock in less than three hours from the time we left Glasgow; and Mr. G. not being arrived, we took up our lodgings in Park's tavern. — That evening we spent in Mr. Park's family, whom I mentioned to you last year, very much to our satisfaction. — Mr. James received us with the affection of a brother, and favoured us much with his company during our stay; a favour that was equally coveted by us all, it being impossible to carry on a conversation with him without receiving information, let the topic be what it will.

Mr. G. joining us next day, we walked out and viewed the environs of the town; and, in the evening, had a party at Park's, consisting of thirteen; where we had an elegant supper, and continued till an early hour, as social, and withal as jovial, as the most sanguine heart could wish. As usual, all was free to us; and we were not a little proud at being honoured with the unexpected company of so many gentlemen of taste and learning; but we missed the ingenious Mr. Galt, who was lately removed to London, and whose absence hath left an irreparable blank in the literary society of Greenock. On the third day, (after breakfasting with Mr. Whitehead) we took leave of our Greenock friends, and set out: keeping along the shore for some miles, we passed through the village of Gourock; and at the Cloch, a good way farther down, took a passage across the Firth. Here our dangers, or at least what we counted dangers, began to commence. We were within a little of being run down by a brig that was coming up the Firth, full before the gale; and were almost under her bow-sprit, when we called out, and the man at the helm, noticing us at a critical moment, put it down, and eschewed us. The swell here was prodigious; even the mariners declared they had scarcely seen the sea so heavy at that season, and the large boat being gone over before us with a carriage, our small wherry wrought terribly. There was a lady, who crossed with us, put up many ejaculations, and often screamed out, when descending from the top of a wave; and even Mr. L. declared, that he had very much ado to keep himself from growing sick, but that he had, however, effected it.

We now landed on Cowal, in the shire of Argyle, I say, *the Shire of Argyle*, for I wish you to take notice when we get out of it. After taking some refreshment at the inn, we entered

◁ Dunbarton Castle

amongst the mountains, intending by night to reach Glendaruel, in the heart of Cowal. But,

"Sic a night we took the road in,
As ne'er poor sinners were abroad in."

For some time, the road kept contiguous to an inlet of the sea, stretching from the Heli-Loch; and on leaving that, in the openings of the glens, were some scenes of inexpressible beauty; scenes which are common enough in Cowal, and peculiar to the Highlands of Scotland. In this district, the detached and broken hills, cloathed in mourning, or otherwise, spotted and shagged like their kindred goats, are, nevertheless, skirted below with sweet-scented birches, spreading hazels, and all the other hardy plants that have been so liberally set by the hand of nature in Scotia's glens; where they spread their simple boughs, and rear their unaffected, yet majestic tops, in defiance of the chill mountain gale, or the boisterous salt-impregnated blast from the Atlantic billows. Here and there a thicket intervenes, where the low entangling sloe-thorn is covered with its snowy robes, and far above it, the aspiring briar bends its slender stem, and nods to the blast; while the wild rose on its top opens its unsullied bosom to the genial rays of the sun; and

courts a sympathetic glance from the eye of the admirer of simple nature.

In some enchanting glades, a pleasant little villa appears, laid out with taste and elegance, the temporary, or constant abode of the curious and wealthy. From the top of the detatched rock, or the abrupt insulated precipice, the black, rugged battlements of ancient castles, fortresses of the feudal chiefs, impending frown on their now mutilated shadows in the briny deep below. These, which in former days were the scenes of blood and stratagem; where oft the intrepid McDonalds resisted for ages the more popular interest and power of the Campbells, though countenanced and backed by royal authority; these, I say, recall to memory the days of ancient times, and naturally influence the mind of the reflecting beholder to compare them with the present. And surely the contemplation, if the balance is impartially hung, must be attended with sentiments of gratitude to that indulgent Benefactor, who controuls universal nature, and in whose hands are all the hearts of the children of men, who hath reversed the picture so much in favour of the present generation. Then the inhabitants of those regions held their properties, and even their lives, on tenures so precarious, that fear kept watch by night, and anxiety pined in listless incertitude during the day. Want soured the temper; and urgent necessity remonstrated to the senses, in terms too pressing to be finally resisted, on the plausibility of committing crimes from which the first ideas started with horror.

Thus the natural bias towards justice and humanity, implanted in the human breast, was gradually over-turned, and every spring of moral purity in the mind tainted and sullied. What was the consequence? ravages! murders! massacres and spoils! Then the most trivial quarrels must be determined by the sword; and hundreds, nay, thousands, were doomed to atone with their blood, for the offended pride, or petty animosity of relentless chiefs; and though faithful and passive to the last degree, their all was subject to every whim and caprice of their superior. How blessed, how happy the change! Now, every man sits under his birk and under his own ash tree, and none to make him afraid. Let the peasant's property be ever so small, now it is his own; and is protected to him from violence. Let his life be of ever so small account, or utility; where is the boldest Peer that now dares attempt to take it away; or even injure his person, though ever so despicable? And, even in this sub-division, of which I began the description, the most predominant feature is never yet mentioned; namely, the low-roofed humble cottages that crowd every shore and opening glen.

There, now, instead of the rapine and terror that once prevailed, love and peace, growing spontaneously up together, nourish and cherish one another: while industry administers to all their wants; and sweet contentment gives full fruition in the enjoyment. Perhaps, you will suppose that I am partial to the cottagers, and exaggerate greatly in ascribing such a share of conjugal felicity, and congenial affection to that humble state. To the former, I plead guilty; but the latter, I will maintain. O my dear Sir! were you as well acquainted with the cottages and their simple inhabitants as I am, which you never will be, you would not suspect the above to be a flattering picture. — Though it must be acknowledged, that in every general rule there are exceptions, and, in none, more than in the temper of man, yet, were I to decide what class of men in the nation enjoyed the greatest share of happiness without alloy, I would, without hesitation, do it in favour of the peasantry.

I have sometimes been admitted to the company and tables of the great, and frequently to those who affect their manners: but the cottage, Sir! the cottage is my native element! No where else is there such a free and unreserved emanation of sentiment, which however homely and ungrammatically delivered, frequently flows from a heart fraught with manly feelings and good natural endowments. There the Sabbath is strictly and conscientiously observed; and there the duties of religion are duly and devoutly performed. Believe me then, Sir, I would rather be the first man amongst the shepherds of Ettrick Forest, than the second in Edinburgh: but the great loss is, that I will never be either the one or the other. As I am rather fallen into a strain too sentimental for writing a journey today, I will bid you farewell.

I am, Yours,

James Hogg

Bellanach
Monday 28th May

Dear Sir, — In my last, I fell into a general description, when losing sight of the firth of Clyde with its numerous branches. We passed Ballachoyle, the valley of Glen-Kin, the house of Armadale, and then crossed a small river without a bridge at the head of Loch-Streven, an arm of the sea which enters the country from the kyles of Bute. It was now growing late, while we had yet another ridge of hills to go over. We were all entire strangers to the country; and the day, which had always been fair at intervals, terminated in a torrent of rain accompanied by a tempestuous wind blowing straight in our faces. Thus we were soon in our usual state, drenched to the skin and mud to the knees; and had nearly precipitated ourselves over a broken bridge in the dark, which would have terminated our journey at once.

At a late hour we reached Glendaruel, in a miserable pickle; and as we had not yet in the least suffered for want of accommodation, we thought our lodging intolerable. It is a large house, and appears to have been a good house, but is badly kept, and quite out of repair: the partitions were full of chinks, by which the wind had free ingress; and the door having no fastening, we were obliged to barricade it with chairs, which was one continual source of uneasiness; and it was not till after two high disputes betwixt Mr. G. and the house that they could be prevailed upon to bring us any fire; alledging as an excuse their extreme scarcity of fuel. When it was brought, our hearts indeed were cheered with agreeable hopes of sometime having a fire and our eyes by a thick piping smoke, but the outward man continued shivering as if in a fit of the ague.

We got as good a supper as the inn could afford; and the fall of rain being nothing abated next morning, we tarried until midday. Mr. L. who is fond of experiments, persuading himself that he had discovered a much more invigorating aliment, and one a great deal more eligible for travellers than those generally used for breakfast, instead of joining us at tea, ordered a dish of paritch, or oatmeal croudy, and porter, to be brought to him, on which he fared sumptuously.

He was our cashier; paid all our bills, freights, and attendants: these last, too, were all commonly left to his discretion, and they of this house, as well as all others who waited for their reward in silent expectation, never had cause to complain.

After taking a short view of the scenery on the banks of Loch-Ruel and the adjacent glen, we mounted the great hill towards the ferry of Ochter on Loch-Fine. As our unlucky stars would have it, some person on the preceding day had been telling me of a nearer road over a hill than the common one; and while ascending this mountain, at a short turn of the road, we perceived a foot-path which led straight over the hill. Not doubting in the least but this was the road I had been informed of, we took to it; though not without violent opposition from Mr. G.; and happy had it been for us all had we hearkened to his voice; for after a rough and fatiguing march, instead of landing at Ochter, we came in upon Loch-Fine opposite to the end of the Crinan canal; when turning to the right, we joined the shore road, which at length brought us to Ochter after having gone many miles about seeking the nearest, on a most tempestuous day.

At Ochter we were obliged to tarry some time, for although the wind was perfectly fair for our passage, being S.E. yet the skipper refused to venture out. Being ushered into a room, we asked for strong ale, which the house at first denied; but seeing that we did not call for anything else, a boy at last came into the room, and creeping into a hole of the wall out of sight, pulled out two or three bottles of it by the neck. I observed to him that

that was the smuggler's hole, which he positively denied. Our ferry-men were at length persuaded to set out, but not until we were obliged to promise them sixpence for each passenger, which were now seven, over and above the common freight. This they charged on pretence that they could not get back that night, and that they would be obliged to pay for their lodging: yet mark the rogues, they were home before we got out of their sight.

Amongst our fellow passengers were two country girls of the better order from Lorn: the day being very rough, we ran down to the dock, and seeing a boat half filled with vernal birks, and not doubting but it was the same in which we should pass, I stepped into it; laid me down on the bieldy side, desiring the prettiest of the girls to take up her birth in my bosom. — She complied without hesitation, and I screened her with my mantle. O! how my companions envied my situation: but when the sailors came, how great was my mortification, to find we had all taken up our stations in a wrong boat. We were all obliged to shift, and I being farthest in, was last in getting out, and lost not only my dearest bosom-friend, but every tolerable seat in the boat, being forced to sit grinning with my face in the weather all the way.

I remember of little more worth mentioning hereabouts. The scenery of the country, as well as the culture, is much the same in the Knapdale side as in Cowal. The hills incline most to heath in appearance, but on a nearer survey are intermixed with a dark-coloured prie, and sundry other salutary herbs. The attention of the farmer is divided too much perhaps to admit of excellence in any one thing, as there are few who possess land to any extent who have not each a share of corn, cattle, and sheep; altho' on the Cowal mountains the sheep are rather the prevailing party. The tillage, which on the shores of Loch-Fine, and in some of the more inland vallies is considerable, consists mostly of detached pieces. Potatoes, bear, and oats, are their only crops; and the latter looked very poorly in the braird.

We had a very agreeable walk to Lochgilphead, for as usual, it rained most furiously. We arrived at the inn in our old state, and though extremely hungry, I thought of nothing but going away without dining, late as it was, such a violent heat arose betwixt Mr. G. and the house. He pretended, as his grounds for this animosity, the huge impropriety of showing us into the bar instead of the dining-room; but the truth of the matter was this: The dialect of the country differed widely from any that he had been acquainted with; and as you know the tone of the voice is understood to be more expressive of the state of mind, and the exact feeling of the speaker with regard to you, than the words which accompany it; so, the sharp key in which they talked, did not accord with the musical ear of my friend, especially the last syllable of each sentence which was not only lengthened out to a minum; but in the beginning also rose to a fifth, and descended with a rapidity, and cadence, so abstracted from all precedent in Italian music, that it raised in him a belief, that the people were not only in a high passion, but treating him with the utmost disdain: and he being resolved to be nothing behind with them, wrought himself into such a strain, that if I had not remained obstinately fixed on my dinner, we had certainly danced off without it.

Here we laid in considerable stores for our voyage, being determined to treat for a passage in the first vessel that left the canal for the north. Accordingly about mid-way we spoke with the *Johnson* of Greenock, bound for the isle of Sky with a valu-able cargo of luxuries: and as the owner made us very welcome to such accommodation as he had, we thought this extremely lucky; but in the event it turned out but moderately so. At a later hour we arrived at Kilmahunock, near the harbour in Loch Crinan, and hard by the entrance from that into the canal, where we called the people from their beds, and took up our lodging. Although this was but a poor despicable inn, the woman was civil and discreet, and we agreed very well.

The next day being Sunday, we were obliged to remain here; as the people will not open the locks to let vessels through on that day, although I wish they may never do a worse turn. Our anxiety to get forward increased with every opposition: and we felt very impatient today, the Monday, which continued so windy, that the vessel could not be moved for fear of being dashed against rocks; while we were cooped-up in our little public house, and could not stir abroad for the rain. On the Sabbath-day we had climbed to the highest point in South Knapdale, from whence we got an extensive view of the Atlant-ic, and of all the islands and headlands that lie between the paps of Jura and the dark rocks that wall the coast of Mull, besides a good extent on the eastern shore of Isla. But as I have described a considerable part of that country already, I shall take my leave, after subscribing myself.

Yours, &c. *Hogg*

Dear Sir, — As it is probable I would mention the house of Bellanach in my former letters, and the improvements carried on there under the auspices of the generous Mr. Malcolm, I shall not run the risk of repetition, but proceed with our voyages. I had, while tarrying here, by my rashness, received a

grievous wound in the face, which I was obliged to keep bound up with a napkin, and which occasioned my having something of a hideous appearance. Wherever I showed my face the people were impressed with high ideas of my prowess in the art of boxing, which I never in my life tried; and I thought it would have been more natural had they concluded that some body had been boxing *me*.

We set sail on the morning of Tuesday with a fine southern breeze, which carried us out of Loch Crinan. About a mile off the point of Craignish we witnessed a very singular phenomenon. A phenomenon, James! little things are such to you when on a journey: pray what was it? Your honour will not guess; not if you should do nothing else but try for a year. It was, however, what I never before saw or heard of; — being a boat well manned, fishing up cows in the open sea. Aye look back at the word again; it is just *Cows.* But I am to this day unable to account for it in the least, or how such a valuable fishery came to be there; but it was literally as follows:

On reaching the sound of Jura, we steered to the northward; where the wind beginning to sink, and the tide meeting us like a mighty river, we advanced very slow. To the westward about half a mile, we first saw a large wherry crouding sail to the South, and then, a good way ahead of her, a black thing came on with the tide, which we soon discovered, with the help of the spyglass, to be an excellent black highland cow. We approached quite near them, and saw them overtake her, when they immediately dropped their sail and threw coils of ropes around her, endeavouring with all their might to haul her into the boat: this however they were unable to effect, for she splashed like a whale; and the boat was like to turn its keel uppermost; but they lashed her to the stern.

Just about this time, when the noise of Gaelic in the boat began to abate, in a moment a dun cow emerged from below the waves about forty yards to the N.W. of us. She was grown very weak, was swimming with her side uppermost, and blowing like a porpoise; but the tide bare her rapidly away from us, and very near straight for them. I cannot describe to you the noise and hurry which ensued in the boat on the appearance of this second prize: some hauled up the sails, others hung strenuously by that which they had got, being unwilling to lose a certainty for a chance. They at last with some difficulty succeeded in securing that also, when they made slowly toward the land.

We were lost in conjecture from whence these cows could have come, there being no other vessel or boat within sight from which they could have made their escape; and could think of nothing more probable, than that they were cattle which had lately been brought from Jura, and were attempting to swim across the sound to their native isle again, a distance I suppose not exceeding eight miles; but you now know as much as I do. After this we continued for some time to hold slowly on our course, but were soon overtaken by a dead calm, when the furious tide carried us straight away to the south.

We were now in no very agreeable situation, being surrounded to the southward by numbers of rocky islets, without any means in our power of eschewing them, and were greatly alarmed at seeing ourselves borne full upon a large one in the mouth of Loch Crinan! the sailors plied with the oars to force the vessel from its longitude, but their efforts for a long time proved abortive. I, for my own part, had no apprehensions of being wrecked on that rock, and strove with all my rhetorick. to persuade them that it was impossible the tide could run us ashore on the island, unless it had a passage under it; for that it must necessarily go about the island itself, and it was plain would carry us with it, especially as its shore did not shelve: and so narrow is my comprehension, that I believe it was the effect of the island's repelling the current that carried us round, and not the oars. A small breeze now coming from the S.W. we stood into the bay of Craignish, and the breeze afterwards increasing, we again beat up, doubled the point of Craignish a second time, and the tide turning in our favours, went on swimmingly.

We kept nearly the same road by which I came last summer, and saw nothing worth remarking saving a great number of fishing boats busily employed on a bank off the slate islands. On the broad channel beyond these islands, and South of Mull, we met with a pretty heavy sea, which was however productive of no worse effect upon any of us, than depriving Mr. W. of the power of speech for about two hours, and covering his complexion with the lily's pallid hue.

As we dreaded again to encounter the tides in the sound of Mull, we came to an anchor in Loch Don, and in company with Mr. McAlister, went and spent the evening at the house of Achnacraig in Mull, which is a good inn, and kept by civil people. Here we tarried until a late hour, and then returned on board our vessel.

There is some green grass surrounding this bay but most of it is upon land which hath been tilled, and is thereby converted from a moss soil into a rich black loam. The mountains are high, the coast, except in the bays, bold and rocky, some brush-wood interlines the declivities; a good way to the eastward appeared the isle of Kerrara, and beyond that the mountains of Lorn; the ruins of Castle-Duart stood on the point beyond us, and upon the whole, the scene was rather interesting, though more so on account of its novelty to us than anything else.

This morning, as soon as it was day, the tide then beginning to ebb, we got under way, the wind being fair and very gentle.

As I did not go to sleep that night, for fear of losing the views, I was on deck all the way, and the morning being fair and clear, enjoyed them very much: my two friends did not awake until we were got up to the narrow sound about the mouth of Loch-Alen. They were much delighted with the wild prospects on each hand, but testified their surprise at seeing so few cottages on coasts, and those that were all in clusters: they seemed also much better pleased with the appearance of the mountains of Mull than those in Morven.

About ten o'clock, we cast anchor in the bay of Tobermory, and went ashore to the village, where Mr. McAllister had some business to transact, but a violent rain commencing, we were forced to keep mostly within doors. Although I did not tarry above two hours at this place last year, and tho' now so much disfigured by the wound in my face, I was surprised at being told by a native who went aboard with us, that the whole village knew me: that they wondered much what my business was there last year, and much more when they saw me return this year: this might possibly proceed from their having a jealousy of strangers, but I rather think that the great number of excise-men on these coasts obliges the highlanders to keep a sharp look out: those of Mull seem to be amongst the most robust, and stout made of any; and many of them wear the old Highland garb, which quite disappears in the country of Lewis and Harris.

Mr. McAlister having settled his business at Tobermory, we left it about 3 o'clock p.m. contrary to the ardent remonstrances of an old sailor named Hugh; and I still believe that our import-unity to get forward influenced the master too much to set out. The wind was now shifted to the West, the day cleared up, and every five minutes the sky wore a more gloomy aspect; the consequence was, that before we passed the bloody bay, where one of the large vessels of the Spanish Armado was ruined, every countenance was stamped with the marks of apprehension; but as it still continued tolerable we held on.

When we reached the point of Ardnamurchan, or the Rhu, as it is commonly called, we were obliged to tack twice in order to weather it, and had already got to the windward of it, when the sea growing prodigiously heavy, and the wind continuing to increase, the sailors were affrighted, and though ten or twelve miles advanced, turned and run again for Tobermory. It was not long until we found ourselves off the mouth of the harbour, but the wind, which was now increased to a gale, blowing straight out of it, and the passage betwixt the island and the rocky point being so narrow that it was dangerous to tack, the getting in became a serious concern: the *Johnson*, though a strong English-built sloop, is certainly the most unwieldy vessel of her size that ever was made. They now made a strong effort to weather the straits, putting her about almost every three minutes; all hands assisted in hauling in the sheets; and after a struggle of nearly two hours, they succeeded in working her through the narrowest, and expected at the next stretch to gain the harbour. There being ten in all on board, and the deck rather throng, I stepped below to prevent confusion and write this letter; but my two companions assisted with all their might, not without imminent danger to their persons, for the boom overthrew Mr. John every time it was dragged in, and very nearly turned him overboard, he not having experience how to manage himself. I was at length alarmed by an unusual noise and bustle above, but still kept tenaciously by my birth in the cabin, until I heard Mr. McAlister cry out in great agitation, O! Lord! she will go in a thousand pieces! — O! my God! my God! cried the man at the helm. Whats the matter now, thought I; and setting my head out at the campeignan door, saw every man rivetted to the spot awaiting his fate in silent horror, In truth, my dear Sir, you need not envy the present feelings of Your most obedient servant

James Hogg

Dear Sir, — I took leave of you in my last at a very alarming crisis, when we were all expecting in a few moments to be plunged in the deep, and in all probability into eternity. The case was thus: We had got within the rocky point which bounds the north side of the harbour, and just when endeavouring to put the vessel about for the last time on that side, a tremendous gale commenced, which threw her so much over, that the main-sail dashed into the sea, and rendered fruitless every effort, not only to bring about the ship, but even to get down the main-sheet in order to let her scud out to sea, clear of the rocks. She was, during the time of this short struggle, driving with great force straight upon the rocks; and the men, not being able to effect anything in the consternation they were in, a moment of awful pause ensued.

Every man quitted his hold, save old Hugh at the helm, and if my chops had not been so much slackened at the inner end, I would have raised the tinker's whistle; when by a singular interposition of Providence, the ship gave a great roll backwards, and the main-sail dropped down of itself, the ropes having been previously loosened, and the vessel whirled round clear of the rocks, tho' within six, or at most, seven yards of them. Old Hugh thanked his Maker aloud for this signal deliverance, and indeed every heart seemed sensibly affected by it. We now stood out to the open sound, intending to weather out the storm without risking the vessel among rocks, to gain a harbour a second time.

It was now wearing late, and I shall never forget the stormy appearance of that awful night: the sun, when about to sink into the waves beyond the isles of Bara, frowned upon us through a veil of pale vapour, and seemed swelled to three times his ordinary size. The atmosphere was all in a ferment, having a thin white scum settled stedfastly on its surface, over the face of which, at short intervals, small clouds flew with amazing velocity. It was not long ere they were convinced that their plan of keeping the sea was impracticable, for, besides that the rigging began to give way, the ship was gradually driving towards the rough coast of Morven. We now steered southward, purposing to try for an anchorage at the green islands in the middle of the sound; this also was rejected as of no avail, and it was determined to turn and run for Loch-Sunart, Donald McEachern of Mull having some acquantance with it.

This Loch-Sunart is a narrow arm of the sea, running about twenty miles into the country, and dividing the districts of Ardnamurchan and Morven. It is a most dangerous place, being all over interspersed with rocks, islands, and narrow rugged points. Towards this place, then, we ran before the wind, depending wholly on Donald, who even confessed that his knowledge of it was but partial: we entered the mouth of it before it was quite dark, and shaping our course for an island that lay about mid-way up, came in sight of it a little after eleven at night. The storm was all this time rather increasing, and such another night I never witnessed at that season, if ever in my life: the elements were in a tumult, and seemed to be taking flame: the pale, vivid bolts, bursting from the rolling clouds, added horror to the scene, and to minds already nearly stupified: the sea seemed covered with sparkling fire, an appearance quite new to us, and which we had no conception of, though we were told it was common in great storms. But Burns shall describe that night, who well can do it:

The wind blew as 'twad blawn its last,

The thickning shower rose on the blast;

The speedy gleams the darkness swallowed, &c.

In the midst of this confusion and anxiety, when we had past several dangerous straits, and were too far gone to retreat, judge of our consternation when we found the wind all at once a turn a-head of us, with still increased violence! while we were in a strange channel which was not clear above a quarter of a mile in any one direction, and at the dead hour of the night, when we could not see from stem to stern. Our condition may be conceived, but cannot be described.

In this situation we turmoiled, beating up until half-past one in the morning, always rather losing ground than gaining, when, at last, in spite of all our efforts, she drove so close upon a rocky isle, that we were obliged, as our last and only resource, to drop the anchors, altho' straight on the weather side of a precipitate rock. The sails were not then got down, and she was swinging about so near the rock, that I could not discern the sea between them; and she passed so near one high point, that I actually offered to leap from the quarter deck, and had certainly perished in the attempt.

After passing this, there was a small creek, about a cable's-length over, before we reached the other rocks, but she still continued to drag the anchors; and when we were again expecting her to go all in shivers — wonderful to relate! when we were so near the rock as to be able to touch it with a staff, the little anchor held. The vessel struck twice; but as the shore was bold, and the anchor continued immoveable, she received little injury. The sailors now gathered double courage, threw the trunks and valuables again out of the boat on board, and cursed, and swore again, as fast as ever. We soon hauled her a good space from the rocks, sent out another anchor by the boat, and tied the hauser to the rocky point which we first so narrowly escaped; when, thinking our danger over, we retired to the cabin, where Mr. McAlister treated us with as much wine as we chose to drink. This cheered again our hearts, and made us talk with kindling ardour on the dangers we had escaped.

I accused my comrades of perplexing the people with questions and advices, when they were already desperate; while they, on the other hand, reprobated me for my indifference, and for taking no more notice of our danger than if such things had not been. We had each of us something to retort upon the other. Mr. William got an hundred falls. Mr. John cut a cable with his razor; and I lost a shoe. But the most interesting figure of the whole group was old Hugh, who had kept the helm from the commencement of the storm. The master, who seemed glad to resign his charge, wrought like the rest of the men in obedience to his orders.

To convey some faint idea of this picture, imagine to yourself a fair complexioned man, about sixty years of age, or upwards, having a blue duffle coat buttoned on him, the tails of which met a little above his knee; and a huge quaker's hat on his head, which he was every minute dashing up with his arm, to drive it from its horizontal direction, and prevent it from intervening betwixt his eyes and the sails, on which they were constantly fixed: his legs were set amazingly wide, in case *Mr. Borcas,* in these freaks of his, might launch him: he was all this while eating tobacco most voraciously, and not having time to spit often, the juice was obliged to find its way from each corner of his mouth in the best manner it could; yet, this was the man who alone remained firm and composed, giving orders and advice with the utmost calmness! his motto being in effect thus, *Let us do our best, and trust to God for the rest.*

After the others went to sleep, I sat up and regaled the crew, after their meal, with whisky, and was delighted to hear old Hugh, after laying aside his broad hat, return thanks to God for his kind interference in our behalf, with the utmost warmth and gratitude. There was another circumstance which occasioned a number of surmises amongst us for some time, and had nearly brought to light several latent sparks of superstition, which, though hereditary, we rather wished to remain dormant.

About the time when we were at the bitterest, just before dropping anchors, we heard the voice of the sand lark upon the adjacent rocks, complaining in rueful notes of our intrusion upon her solitude at that untimely season of the night. Whilst a voice so familiar to us countrymen, conveyed a kind of melancholy pleasure our ears were saluted all at once with an elderich broken shriek, as if uttered by a person in the utmost desperation: in a few seconds it was again repeated, and we heard no more. As soon as we got time to reflect, we concluded that it had been some person who had eyed our distress from the shore, and was crying aloud to warn us of certain destruction, if we did not avoid that place; but on discovering that it was an uninhabited island, we could father it upon nothing but the angry spirit of the waters. Next day, however, as some of us were traversing the rock, we started a few goats, which cleared up the mystery, it being evident that the noise from the vessel had scared them, and their bleating, echoed by the rocks, had been that which alarmed us. That day we were visited by several boats from Morven; two of these arrived before sunrise, pretending that they thought the vessel wrecked, and lying on the rocks, and wished to render us what assistance they could; we suspected their motives to be quite different, but perhaps we judged wrong. We remained on board and on the island all that day, and the following night; but on the morning of the second day, the wind still continuing boisterous from the N.W. which rendered it impossible to get out the ship, we were obliged, reluctantly, to take leave of the *Johnson* and Mr. McAlister, and endeavour exploring our way on foot through the pathless mountains of Ardnamurchan and Moidart, towards the kyles of Sky. This Loch-Sunart, and its environs, is a very wild scene, and though not destitute of beauty, it is rather of the savage kind, being a group of precipitate rocks, green hallows, and wild woods; with the sea winding amongst them in every direction; and the back ground shaded by a range of black-topped mountains, embosomed in which the mean hamlets lie hid from all the rest of the world.

I am, dear Sir,

Your ever faithful servant,

Mr. Eltrich Shepherd

139

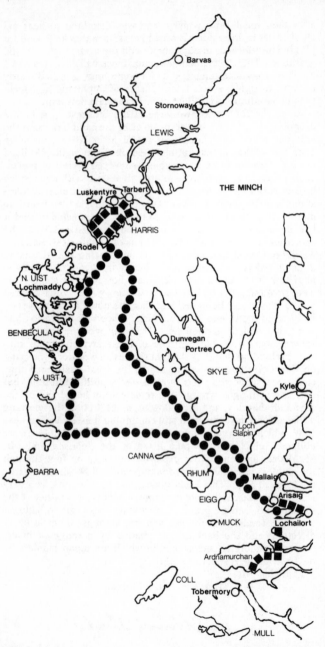

Dear Sir, — I said in my last, that it was with reluctance we took leave of Mr. McAlister, nor was it any wonder, for it was impossible we could have met with a sea-faring man better fitted to make our voyage agreeable; had we not been so much harrassed by -

"Tempests themselves, high seas, and howling winds,

The gutter'd rocks, and congregated sands,

Traitors ensteep'd to dog the guiltless keel,"

we had certainly enjoyed his company very much; for besides having the ship stored with all the good things of this life, he had an excellent chart of the coast, a perspective glass, and a good violin, on which we could all perform a little, and also Ossian's poems, Burns's works, and several books of taste: his manners were simple and unaffected, and his nature kind and affable, and he certainly may be ranked amongst the first of merchants.

We mounted the braes of Ardnamurchan at the farm house of Borrowdale, by a small foot track that soon evanished. Here there are many green patches amongst the woods and alongst the shore, but higher on the hills, the soil is wholly moss, and the vegetable productions heather and ling.

In ascending this hill, we were rivetted to a certain spot a good while, listening to the most mellifluous music, which came floating on the breeze from a neighbouring wood, sometimes in a cadence so soft and low as scarcely to be heard, and at other times in full concert, so loud that all the hills rang again. This proceeded from a great number of people, of both sexes, who were cutting and peeling wood at that place; and being assembled at their breakfast, had joined in singing a Gaelic song, in the chorus of which they all joined: and though their notes were wild, and, as we thought, irregular, yet by reason of the distance, and the fine echo of the woods and rocks, the effect was excellent.

With some difficulty we found our way over the height, and came in view of Loch-Moidart in Inverness-shire: and what added not a little to our vexation, no sooner had we got over the rough hedge, and spied out the way by which we proposed to get forward, than the wind shifted to the South, and the rain commenced; so that if we had stayed two hours longer in the ship, we had soon been landed in Sky, where I was acquainted.

We now went through a stock of good short sheep belonging to a Captain Cameron, whose house we passed by, for fear we should have been suffered to tarry in the kitchen, our cloathes being now much soiled on board; but even in the most trivial things we were unlucky; going a nearer way, as we thought, above the house, we came upon precipices and ravines so inaccessible, that it was with difficulty we reached the shore hard by the house, after all our trouble. A little after this, the tide being in, we run ourselves within a long narrow arm, by which it run up into the country, and were obliged to wade through it above our middle in salt water: being now uncertain by which way to proceed, we called at a poor cottage where a little girl, having some English, showed us the road for Island - Teona, in Loch-Moidart, by which it was necessary we should pass. After this we were entangled in a morass of prodigeous extent, quite level, and only a little elevated above the sea, and so soft and miry, that when we leaped from one place covered with a scurf to another, to avoid sinking, it would shake and heave to the distance of a rood around us; and we certainly were in more danger than we were aware of, for we were afterwards told that no person attempted crossing through the middle of it where we went.

After passing a number of poor cottages in a cluster, we came unto the beach opposite the house of Island-Teona, where making a sign for a boat, two fine boys, sons to Mr. McDonald of that place, came and rowed us over to their fathers' house, where they entreated us to enter, where we were hospitably entertained with the best the house could afford. Here we were joined by one Mr. Macallum, an exciseman of that country, who accompanied us all the way to Arisaig. Mr. McDonald caused his sons to row us round the island, and land us on the mainland in the country of Moidart. On our way we passed by a natural canal, so narrow, that there was scarcely room to work the oars, and saw the mighty ruins of Castle Tuirim, which they said was formerly the residence of Macdonald of Clanranald. We now climbed the mountains of Moidart, and in less than two hours came in upon the shore of Loch Nanuach, an arm of the sea about six or seven miles broad.

It was all this time raining incessantly, and we were, as usual, as wet as water could make us; but to embitter our state a little further, the wind was now grown so rough that the ferry-men would in no-wise venture out, and there being no place there where four of us could lodge, we were forced to turn alongst the shore to the eastward by the most terrible road of all: rapid torrents, flooded by the rain, came rushing and roaring from the mountains; these we were obliged to stem, and climb over numerous precipices on all fours. We at length reached the genteel house of Ewrin, where we were again entertained by Mr. McEchern, who entreated us to stay all night, but perceiving that we wished to get forward, procured us a boat and crew to carry us over. The boat being small, and crouded, and the sea very rough, we were certainly in considerable danger; the waves often washing over her, threatened to suffocate us with brine; the man at the rudder however always bid us fear nothing, and, to encourage us, sung several Earse songs.

We passed several small islands, on one of which there is a vitrified fort, and we came to the very creek where the unfortunate Prince Charles Stewart first landed on the mainland of Scotland in the year 1745. Yea, the people told us a thing of much importance, that we even stepped out upon the very same rock which he stepped out upon, and shewed us the cottage where he and his few companions lodged that night, on which occasion that song, called the *"Eight men of Moidart,"* was composed: the same woman who entertained them still resides on the spot, though now in somewhat of a better house. After again walking over some low hills, we came to a good road, which led us to the village of Arisaig, where there is a good inn, at which we arrived ere it was quite dark, and were comfortably lodged.

The country hereabouts had a more promising appearance than the banks of Loch-Moidart; the hills were moderately high, and towards the coast low, and mixed with spots of arable ground, not unfertile, altho' badly tilled, and their ridges formed after the pattern of the new moon. In all these districts the sheep stocks were well attended to, and the breeds were, on many farms, above mediocrity: they are all of the blackfaced breeds, and some of the smaller farmer's stocks retain too striking marks of their consanguinity to the old degenerate highland breed. Smearing with tar and grease is becoming more general, but even those which we saw unsmeared were not much ragged in their fleeces: the frost there is never very intense, when the salt-impregnated vapours are unfavourable to the breeding of vermin upon them. There are likewise large herds of black cattle, but amongst the better sort of farmers or tacksmen, these are yearly losing ground.

The coast to the north of this, as well as that which we had passed, being all indented by extensive arms of the sea, and these divided by pathless mountains, we found it impracticable, in such unseasonable weather, to proceed to Glen-Elig on foot as we at first proposed; and it was necessary, either to hire a boat to carry us to Slate, in Sky, then traverse that country to Dunvegan; and there again take chance of a passage from that to Rowdal in Harris; or else hire a boat in this place to carry us there, wait our return, and bring us back again. We very soon agreed that the latter was most expeditious, as well as the most convenient and genteel way of travelling.

We accordingly hired a tight schooner, named *the Hawk of Oban,* and embarked today about noon. Our bargain with the owners is that they are to set us down on any part of Harris we choose, where they are to wait our return and bring us back to Arisaig. Our crew consists of two brothers, stout young lads, who are the owners of the vessel, and another man whom they hired.

We left Arisaig, as I said, about noon, giving them directions

143

to steer for Ensay in the sound of Harries, or else for Island-Glass in Loch-Tarbet, distant from this place about an hundred miles. We found our way out of Loch-Arisaig, or Loch-Nakeane, by a long intricate passage, stretching southward, leaving an innumerable range of insulated rocks on our starboard side; and, by the bye, this is certainly as dangerous a bay as is on these coasts, if the mariners are not minutely acquainted with it. *The Hawk*, though a fine sailer, and easily managed, drew very little water, and was uncommonly light and ticklish; therefore, when the sea was heavy or rough, she wrought and rolled most violently; and as soon as we were got into the open channel, the airy motion began to affect the stomachs of my two friends; but as the breeze was gentle, instead of sickening them, on the contrary, it only created the most voracious appetite for food. We have some victuals on board, but none ready cooked; and as there is no appearance of kindling a fire, Mr. John soon grew quite desperate, and began to look first over the one shoulder and then over the other, as not knowing what to do. Our sailors having very little English, I thought I should have perished with laughing, when I saw him, with a famished look, go and implore them for a piece of bread in the most correct English he was master of, that they might by no means misunderstand him. I will tell you how he fares in my next.

I am yours, &c.

Loch Madi   North Uist
Sunday 3rd June

Dear Sir, — I took leave of you in my last when we were hovering to the N.E. of the isle of Egg, and suffering the most poignant throes of hunger. "Sirs, "have you ainy bridd?" said Mr. J. "Hu, she, she," said Angus. "I wish you would gie me a small piese," returned he. Angus either did not understand, or took no notice of him, for the request was never granted. — The worm continued to gnaw. "There will be nothing for it," said I, "but to eat oakum and drink bilge water;" "Faith," said Mr. W., "we'll lick meal and eat cheese." "L—d preserve us," said Mr. J. Angus now struck up a good fire, and put on a pot full of ugly ill-washed potatoes, with six salt herrings. I have seen the day when Mr. W. would have thought them next to poison; but he now started a doubt that they were not meant for us, as they really did not belong to us; this was a piece of heavy news, and I strove to corroborate it by unanswerable evidence. "I believe it is the case," said Mr. J., "but 'tis no matter, we

144

must just mutiny, and take them by force, for I can put off no longer:" "d—n them," said W. "If they don't give us their potatoes, we'll give them none of our gin." We were, however, invited to partake of this delicious fare, "and snapt them up, baith stoop an' roop:" we began at the tails of the herrings, and ate them off at the nose, leaving nothing but the two eyes.

We continued to move slowly on, and got some striking views of Egg, which hath a very romantic appearance from some points, especially from the N.W.; on the other hand, the stupendous mountains of Coulan in the forest of Sky, with some of the bold promontories of that island, formed a scene of the wildest grandeur. As we approached the coast of Rum, we saw four or five whales playing in the mouth of the bay, one of which was amongst the largest of them that frequent those seas. In the evening we were quite becalmed a little off the north-east coast of Rum, when we retired all three to our hammocks, and slept soundly until about two in the morning; when I got up, being somewhat disgusted at having arrested an overgrown louse which was traversing one side of my beard: it was then beginning to blow fresh out of the S.W. and a dark fog hid everything from our eyes.

As I perceived the direction of Cannay when I arose, I expostulated with the men on the impropriety of holding so far to the southward, but they were inflexible, and held on their course. The wind again increased to a gale; the sea grew rough, and the vessel rolled amain. It was on the morning of the Sabbath, and I shall never forget the impatience manifested by Mr. W. on awaking and perceiving our condition; he spoke none; his colour was as pale as if the cold hand of death had been upon him; and his mouth had assumed an exact resemblance in shape to a long bow, the nether lip being the string. He came running out of the forecastle, and placed himself beside me astern; arose that moment, and run again into the forecastle; tumbled over every thing that came in his way; hasted back again to me. I said he would hurt himself. What was it that hurried him so? Nothing, nothing," said he, "only I have some potatoes roasting in the fire, and I am afraid they will burn." He was by this time growing extremely sick, and knew not well what he said; I perceived this, and a little after asked him how he did? He returned me the following laconic answer, in words scarcely articulate, "O Sir, I'm gone!"

The motion of the vessel had also by this time thrown Mr. J. into a morbid lethargy; he still kept his hammock, and puked at times so violently, that I thought his chest should have rent. The fog still continued, and we saw no land until about seven o'clock, a.m. Had our crew steered in the direction they ought to have done, we should by this time have been in the sound of Harris; and tho' I easily perceived that they were luffing too much, I had hopes that we would land somewhere in that neighbourhood. What then was our Mortification, on perceiving that we were off Boigdale-head in South Uist, a short way north of the Sound of Barra; and that after having sailed about thirty hours, to find that we were no nearer our destination than when we set out from the mainland the preceding day!

They could make no apology for this mistake, but only, that they foresaw a storm, and wished to reach a coast on which they could find shelter in case of necessity. They had certainly considerably mistaken their bearings; but the truth was, that they were utter strangers on the coasts of Harries, although one of them pretended to the contrary; and they wished not to approach it on any account, but, at all events, not until the weather mended.

My two friends continued all this while excessively sick: Mr. J. lay in a drowsy insensibility, callous and indifferent either to danger or disappointment. He manifested, however, not the least dissatisfaction; and whenever I asked him how he did, his answer was always, "I am quite well, now."

This was not the case with Mr. W., who was continually shifting the scene. Now he would be lying on his lowly couch, groaning and vomiting: anon, he would be on deck taking the sailors to task; but as they did not understand his dialect, he frequently left them in a huff, and retired again to his hammock. I never heard him receive a satisfactory answer, save one, and then, though they were at cross purposes, they were both satisfied. "Is that South Uist, or North Uist?" said he, pointing to the shore, and meaning the isles of S. and N. Uist. "It is South Uist, Sir," said Angus, "look at the compass." His stomach heaved so much, that his chest would not dilate to take in more air than was sufficient for the utterance to two or three words; and as he was continually engaged in swallowing, or endeavouring to swallow his spittle, his sentences were very short and comprehensive. Whenever I asked him how he did, his answer was uniformly "O Gud!" After a breathing he would sometimes add, — "this is terrible work." Though there are few of the human race whom I respect more than this gentleman, as judging him every way worthy of it, yet I can scarce help laughing, when I think now of how he was horrified at the sea storm.

We now run before the wind with great velocity, keeping in a straight line with the headlands of South Uist, Benbecula, and North Uist, for upwards of fifty miles. The whole of these coasts presented nothing to our eyes but naked desolation: the sea seems to have washed away everything but the solid rocks, and to have forced itself into the country in innumerable creeks, in spite of every other impediment. The predominant colour on the face of the Uists is that of the grey rock, and where soil of any kind prevails, it is only a turf of moss. On the western shore, indeed, there are a few bays, around which there is a mixture of sand, where crops are raised equal to any in these barren regions. The coasts are bold and rocky, but low in comparison with those of Sky. We looked into Loch-Eynard, when we were first certified where we were; and I could scarcely prevent the sailors from running into it for shelter, as I never could apprehend any danger while we were on a weather shore, and plenty of sea-room. About mid-day we opened Loch-Madi in North Uist, when no arguments could move them to proceed further; so they run the vessel up into it, and anchored beside other two large ones that had taken shelter there. It is not easy to conceive a more dreary and dismal-looking scene, than the environs of this harbour exhibit: the whole country is covered with moss, or grey stones, without the smallest green spot; the sea runs into the country nearly the whole breadth of the island, and spreads itself into a thousand branches, stretching in every direction, which renders travelling completely impracticable; and indeed there is not the smallest semblance of a road. We were, however, agreeably surprised at finding a good slated inn, of two stories, where we took up our residence during the remainder of the day, and the following night.

I continue, Sir, as usual, Your affectionate,

Eldrick Shepherd

Balnachulish
Wednesday 13th June

Dear Sir, — After having detained you so long reading a voyage, which, though rendered somewhat interesting by the many cross dispensations attending it, is, nevertheless, trifling, and fraught with very little information, I shall hasten to a conclusion, or at least to places which I have not heretofore visited.

You would lose all patience, were I to detail the whole of our adventures in Uist, which are nevertheless well worthy of a place; and if you had not found fault with me in this respect, you should have heard such a story! What should I have heard, James? You should have heard what a curious waiter we had; — how he clasped his hands above his head whenever he could not comprehend our meaning; — how much we were at a loss for want of Gaelic; — how we hunted the rabbits; — tired of waiting at Kersaig, and set out to traverse the country on foot to its northern extremity, and there procure a passage for Harries. You should have heard our unparalleled embarrassments and difficulties, and how we fell out with the natives and were obliged to return; — how we arrived again at the place where we set out in the morning, both completely drenched and fatigued; — how the house, and every part about it, was crowded with some hundreds of Lord Macdonald's people, who were assembled to pay their rents; — what an interesting group they were, and how surprised my two friends were at seeing such numbers in a place which they had judged a savage desert, and unfit for the nourishment of intellectual life. You should likewise have heard how our crew fell asleep on board, and could not be awakened; — of Donald's despair: and many other interesting particulars, of which you must now live and die in ignorance.

We at length left Loch-Madi with a fair wind, and, in two hours, found ourselves in the great bason at Rowdil in Harries, which is one of the greatest curiosities in these countries. There are three narrow entrances into it, but the middle one is impassible, and very dangerous to strangers, as it is the only one which is seen; and had not the inhabitants of Rowdil observed us in a critical minute, *we* had infallibly been dashed to pieces, as we were entering it in full sail: but they, joining in a general shout, tossed their bonnets up into the air, and thus opened our eyes to our imminent danger; nor was it with small difficulty that we then got the vessel put safely about, on the very brink of the sunk rocks. A pilot soon after arriving, we got safely in by the south entrance, and lodged that night at the inn in the village of Rowdil, where we got plenty of everything, and were well refreshed. Here we all manifested considerable satisfaction at having gained in safety the place to which we were bound, after having struggled so long with conflicting elements.

As I made considerable stay here the preceding summer, it is probable I would describe this place in a former letter, therefore I shall only tell you in this, that we travelled from Rowdil to Luskintyre on foot, a distance of twelve miles; there we tarried three days, which we spent in traversing the country, viewing it minutely as far as the isthmus of Tarbet.

We visited several of the cottages and shealings, contemplating their manners, and modes of tillage. We were treated in an original stile by some of the inhabitants; and in one cottage, surprised half a score of females plying at the fulling of cloth, and braying a song with a vehemence which seemed the effect only of madness or inspiration; and though there were four of us, exclusive of a servant, all more genteelly dressed than those they were wont to see, and all strangers, yet they were nothing abashed; on the contrary, the mania seemed rather to gather new vigour, and I am not certain if any of them even deigned to look at us, As I have nothing new to offer on the present state of farming of this country, I shall cease to entertain you with adventures and anecdotes where I have a mixture of nothing else. Suffice it then to say, that after a stay of three days at Luskintyre, we travelled again to Rowdil by another way, keeping the eastern side of the island, than which a more barren

148

and inhospitable scene is not to be met with in the highlands, being wholly covered with rocks, moss, and stagnant lakes. Arriving at Rowdil, we tarried there another night, and the next morning hoisted sail and departed again for Arisaig.

Having been detained such a weary time on our journey to Harries, my two friends were grown quite impatient to return home; and I was obliged, reluctantly, to come away with them, without seeing either Ensay or Mr. Hume; although a messenger arrived at Luskintyre with a pressing invitation for us to join them, with which, if I had been suffered to comply, a great part of my ensuing misfortunes had been prevented: so unqualified is human prudence to judge what may be the consequences of the smallest or most favourable incidents, for what I here viewed as my greatest happiness in this journey, namely their company, turned out my greatest bane.

We left the coast of Harries with a fair wind, which bye and bye grew considerably rough; and the *Hawk* being so buoyant, by the time we were off Dunvegan-head in Sky, my two friends were again seized with severe qualms, which continued during the rest of our course. Mr. J., who had hitherto been quite calm and resigned, now became somewhat frenzical, and though he slept for the most part, he would sometimes come on deck, and maintain a point was contesting with him. As for Mr. W. he always continued in a state of utter despair, from the time that the vessel began to rock, viewing our fate as certain, and our escape rather a miracle, if it should happen; and whatever he saw or talked of, his thoughts were wholly engrossed by them cursed winds and waves, in whose power we had put ourselves so entirely.

"There is a body of our friends again," said he once, meaning the marrots; "I see they are still persisting in their old plan of drinking:" his looks shewed that his heart had no share in the observation.

Off the mouth of Loch-Slapan we were overtaken by a dead calm in the very place where the meeting of tides carried the most dreadful swell that ever I witnessed. I never felt more disagreeable all the way than I did here, for the space of ten minutes; but it originated wholly in idea, for the sea-sickness never infected me in the least. Mr. J. was lying in his hammock when it commenced, and being unwilling to move, his feet he placed against one place, and his shoulders to another, resolved to keep his birth per force; but all his endeavours proved fruitless, he was tossed out. He then set up his bare head, which was all in an uproar, out at the hatch. "What now, Sirs? What now," said he. "L—d preserve us, what's the matter now?" The mast was at this time alternatively striking on the waves on each side, and the men were apprehensive that it should be torn from the beam. In a short time, however, the breeze again set in, and bore us safely into Arisaig, where we dined, and that

evening travelled to Kinloch-Enort a stage on the road to Fort William.

When we arrived there the people were all in bed, but on rapping loudly at the door, the landlord, a big black, terrible-looking fellow, came stark naked, and let us in: he then lighted a candle, tied on his kilt, and asked how far we had come today. We told him from Harries. He stared us full in the faces, and perceiving that we were in our sober senses, answered only with a hem! as much as to say, I know how you should be believed. He then shewed us into a little damp room with an earthen floor and set before us what cheer he had in the house for supper, which consisted of cakes, milk, and rum, for what is very strange, he had no whisky. In this same apartment there were two heather beds without hangings, on one of which a woman and some children were lying. Mr. W. was now in a terrible passion, and swore he would abandon that horrid place, and take shelter in the woods. The woman and children, however, slid away; the beds were made up with clean cloathes, and we were obliged to pass the night on them the best way we could.

Mr. L. complained much in the morning of several rude engravings made on his body by the stubborn roots of the heather and Mr. G.'s back was all tamboured work but I, by being forced to take to the bed which the family had left, got the advantage of a feather bed among the heath.

Proceeding on, we passed Loch-Shell, and rested and refreshed ourselves at Lochiel-Head; and so on by the shore of that extensive inlet of the sea, until we came to the embryo of the Caledonian canal, at which a great number of people were employed; but, at that early season, the advance they had made was not great; and I acknowledge, that while observing how carelessly the labourers were dabbing with their picks and spades, and how apt they were to look around them at every thing which was to be seen; while others were winding slowly out with each a little gravel in a wheelbarrow, — I say, while contemplating the exertions of these men, and wishing to anticipate in my mind the important aera when they would join Lochiel to the Moray Firth at above fifty miles distance, I would not help viewing it as a hopeless job: my head grew somewhat dizzy, and I felt the same sort of quandary as I used to do formerly when thinking of eternity. It was, on the other hand, creative of a joyous sensation, as it pourtrayed in lively colours the beneficence of our government, and its kind concern about everything that can contribute to the happiness of a brave people, and the prosperity of this too long neglected country.

This road by which we had come from Arisaig is all tolerably good, saving about three miles in the middle, which is nearly impassible; and as it is much the nearest communication be-

◁ Loch Shiel and Glenfinnan monument

twixt the south country and the extensive and populous isles in the shires of Inverness and Ross, the rendering of it a safe and easy passage for horses and carriages, is certainly a matter of much national utility. On all this track the country is finely calculated for producing the finer breeds of sheep, the grounds being so remarkably well sheltered. I am no mineralogist, but there appears to be something peculiar in the stones of this glen. There are numberless stratas in the rocks, of a hard crystaline nature, which, when exposed to the weather, degenerate into a horny and flexible substance, capable of being parted into the most thin transparent slices imaginable. These, one would imagine on viewing, the fire would consume in a moment; but, on the contrary, it makes no impression on them.

After this, we crossed the river at Inverlochy; and, about five o'clock, p.m. arrived at Fort William, intending to tarry there all night; but, unfortunately for us, as well as many others, no doubt, the lady of Glencoe, an amiable young woman, of the most respectable connections, had been lately carried off by an unfortunate accident, and that was her burial day: and as the northern gentry were all expected to tarry in the village on their return from the burial place in Loch-Leven, there was not one of the houses would admit us as lodgers: and Mr. W. got into such a passion at the people's impertinence, that he would not suffer us to take any dinner, for fear lest the abominable town should be benefited by our money; nor would he listen to the arguments, that we were only taking amends of ourselves; which, considering the state of our stomachs at that time, was ample enough.

Mr. J. however, wisely tarried behind, and bought some sweet-meats, which he distributed amongst us, else I know not how we should have endured the other stage of fourteen miles. We passed some scenes of incomparable beauty; cottages embosomed in wild woods, and hallows of the hills; and at a late hour arrived, weary and fatigued, at Balnachulish, where I shall bid you good-night, after subscribing myself,

Your affectionate Shepherd,

James Hogg

Yarrow
Saturday 16th June

Dear Sir, — I took leave of you in my last at Balnachulish, near which, there is abundance of excellent slate; and crossing over the ferry in the morning, we bad farewell to Lochaber, and entered the famous vale of Glencoe, rendered so by the base

◁ Loch Leven from Ballachulish Ferry

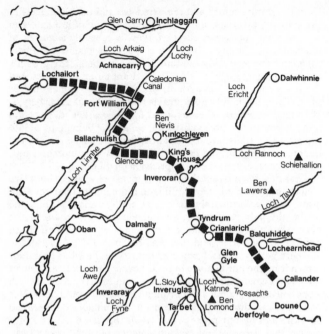

and cowardly slaughter of the Macdonalds in 1691; and also for the extraordinary ruggedness and terrific majesty of the mountains overhanging it on each side. Perhaps there is no one place in Glencoe, taken separately, that may not be equalled, and even surpassed by other parts of Scotland; but taken altogether, it is certainly a scene of the most horrid grandeur that is anywhere to be met with in the British dominions. Such an accumulation of the awful and sublime can hardly be conceived. It is also supposed by some who are versed in the Gaelic etymology, that this was the birth-place of the poet Ossian; and that the river is the Cona so much celebrated in these songs of ancient times; and, indeed, the names of several of the adjacent mountains seem to warrant such a conjecture.

You will observe, my dear Sir, that I have no doubts respecting the existence of the bard; but whether his heroes had any, save in his brain, may perhaps turn out a point that will admit of discussion. Glencoe is, however, stocked with excellent sheep, that is what we are sure of; but it is hard now to discern where so many people could have resided in the glen, as seem to have lived there previous to the revolution.

The day was very hot, and we arrived at the Kings' house, in the Black mount, almost parched with thirst. — "Have you any porter?" said Mr. L. on entering — "haneal," said the wife,—

"And ale?" said he — "oh! that's very good." We were very sorry to find she had answered in Gaelic, and that she had neither the one nor the other. She had, however, plenty of tea, the only beverage in the Highlands that a stranger can partake of freely. We then came over the Black mount. Rested at Inverouran; and after crossing the Orchay, and the beautiful extensive sheep farm of Auch, arrived in the evening at Tynedrum; an excellent inn in that district of Breadalbin, called Strathfillan, where the great lead mines are situated. From thence we departed next morning, and in our way saw St. Fillans, or the Holy Pool; and I took occasion to question a farmer, a native of that place, concerning that extraordinary superstition.

But how astonished was I to hear, that even in this enlightened age, it was as firmly believed in as ever! yea to hear its infallible efficacy attested with great warmth; and numberless late instances adduced as unanswerable evidences. It is just a common pool in the water of Fillan, the topmost branch of the great river Tay, and bears an exact resemblance, in every respect, to a pool high on Tweed, called the Wisdom Pool, and which, I am persuaded, hath formerly been used for the same purpose. This pool the inhabitants believe to be supernaturally endowed with an extraordinary quality on a certain returning

day each quarter of the year, and on these days, all the people, both far and near, that are in any degree deranged in their minds, are brought to it as a certain restorative.

Beside the pool is an altar, or rather cairn of stones, on which an offering is first laid with great reverence to St. Fillan, the tutelary Saint of the country, by whose agency this miracle is brought about; after that, the patients are tumbled into the pool over head and ears; then pulled out dropping wet; bound hand and foot with strong ropes, and locked up in the chapel, where they are suffered to remain until the sun rise next morning. If they are found then bound in the same manner as when left the preceding day, it is looked on as a bad omen, and they are carried home with wailings, because their offerings have not been accepted: but Mr. R— C—, my informer, assured me, that this did not happen above once in seven years; for though you bound them with all the ropes in Strathfillan, they would be loosed in part next day.

He also assured me, that there were numbers thus bathed and were bound every year; and I found, on conversing with a south-country man who resided there, that its good effects were so visible, that it was allowed, by the most sensible people of the place, to contribute much to the recovery of such as were thus affected.

The latter also told me, that he once saw seven ducked all at once, one of whom was a weaver, who was as much knave as fool. This fellow declared afterwards, that he, with a great deal of difficulty, disengaged himself, and afterwards loosed all the rest.

It is certainly not a little remarkable that this superstitious belief should prevail in an enlightened country, so late as the present day; and as no person can now have any interest in carrying it on as a trick, it can only be accounted for from some experience of its efficacy. This then must certainly be accounted for in some more natural way than the supernal virtues of its water on such days; and it is beneficial to persons thus afflicted, which is at least dubious, any day of the year, and any pool and chapel will do as well as these of St. Fillan; or otherwise, it is a very well-contrived plan to work on the imagination.

After this, we turned down Glendochart; rested at Sui; and then mounted the hills, by a foot path, into the braes of Balquhidder. From the height, we had a fine view of Loch Tay, and the mountains of Breadalbin, several of which are amazingly high, and specked with eternal snow. Ben-Lawers, supposed the highest of the range, properly called the Grampians, is elevated upwards of 4,000 feet above the sea. Ben-More, Ben-Leo, and Ben-Doran, are all said to be below that height, but very near it. The whole of Breadalbin, with its adjacent glens, is an excellent sheep country, and it being the first on which the improved breed of short sheep was tried, it hath long produced large droves of the best wedders, most of which are bred at home; yet the draft ewes which that country sends to the south, are commonly of an inferior quality. This must either be owing to their age, or bad treatment, as it is evident from the samples of their wedders what the country can do. The Earl of Breadalbin now sets his pasture farms very high, some of them being, by computation, five shillings and nine-pence for each sheep. It abounds with a variety of scenes of great natural beauty.

We now descended into the country of Balquhidder, the hills of which are inferior to none in the Highlands for sweet natural pasture-ground. You are better acquainted with that country than I am, and also with the finely contrasted scenery on the banks of Loch-Lubnich, of which we got a good view as we passed along.

Afterwards, passing through Callander, we slept that night at Down; and the next day, taking seats in the Stirling fly, we returned by Edinburgh and Peebles into Ettrick-Forest.

As you have travelled all these roads in idea with me former-ly, I shall not take up your time, and my own much longer, in detailing the other trifling adventures we encountered by the way. We arrived in Yarrow precisely in five days from the time of our leaving Harries. — Thus terminated the *unfortunate journey,* as it is generally called. Nor will you refuse your assent to the propriety of the denomination, when you consider that it was not productive of one good effect: that we never, in our way out, walked an hour without being drenched to the skin, and mudded to the knees: that we never went to sea, though but for a few miles, without encountering storms, accidents, and dangers: nor even, after leaving Greenock, proceeded one day by the route we intended, but either lost our way by land, or were thwarted by the winds and the sea. Yea, so visibly were we crossed in the very smallest matters, that the latent sparks of superstition, believed to be inherent in our countrymen, were aroused; and we all three concluded, that an over-ruling Provid-ence frowned upon our designs; and the event hath now fully justified the prediction.

Now, my dear Sir, acknowledge that I have ful-filled your injunctions to a tittle, in giving you an account of my Highland journies; and as I am resolved never more to take another journey, of such a nature, at my own expence, and it is most probable no other will employ me, so I expect this will be the last letter ever you will receive from me on these subjects. I will therefore take my leave, with assuring you, that I remain

Your most affectionate, Obliged and faithful Shepherd,

James Hogg

INDEX

◁ St. Mary's Loch Yarrow